How to use this workbook

Structure

The activities in this workbook will help you to develop the skills and knowledge that you will need to achieve your best grade in A-level English Literature, whichever exam board specification you are following.

Each section offers a clear structure with activities that gradually increase in difficulty:

- **Starting out:** accessible activities that offer an introduction to the topic.
- **Developing your ideas:** skills-building activities that look in more detail at particular aspects of the text.
- **Taking it further:** more challenging tasks that will test your understanding of the text and consolidate your learning.

Boosting your skills

The final chapter of the workbook offers exam-focused activities that allow you to apply the skills you have developed. It also includes step-by-step guidance on the Assessment Objectives, and how to cover them in your written responses.

Features

Key terms

Definitions of key concepts and terminology. Understanding these and using them correctly in your written responses will help gain marks.

Key skills

Concise explanations of important skills to develop during your A-level studies. A variety of skills are covered, from fundamental ones such as analysing the structure of a text or embedding quotations in your writing, up to more advanced skills that are necessary to gain the top grades, such as exploring different interpretations of characters.

Challenge yourself

Advanced tasks that will push you further and help prepare you to achieve your best grade in the exams. They often focus on context (AO3), connections between texts (AO4) or critical interpretations of them (AO5).

Answers can be found at: **www.hoddereducation.co.uk/workbookanswers**

Introduction

Measure for Measure speaks strongly to twenty-first century audiences: it combines comedy and tragedy, presents complex ambiguities and explores moral issues that are still current. No one who has heard of the allegations against Harvey Weinstein will think that the sexual exploitation of women by powerful men was just a seventeenth-century phenomenon.

Studying *Measure for Measure* at AS/A-level and using this workbook

Your study of Shakespeare for GCSE is a good basis for approaching *Measure for Measure* for AS/A-level. You need to develop and extend your existing skills alongside a more detailed understanding of the text, the context and a range of critical approaches. Activities in this workbook have been designed to support you in this process. You will encounter perspectives from a range of critics and other readers to help you to develop your own response to the play. You will also consider the social, historical and cultural/literary contexts of *Measure for Measure*, and how these influenced the play.

You will still need to study characterisation and themes at A-level, but you will be expected to have a deeper awareness of how these aspects function and are presented. The sections on 'Themes' and 'Characterisation' will help you to refine your appreciation of Shakespeare's craft as a playwright and how he presents his characters and develops his key ideas and concerns dramatically.

An important skill for students of literature is the ability to analyse the **ways** meanings are shaped through Shakespeare's methods. Activities in both the 'Plot and dramatic structure' and 'Writer's methods: Language and style' sections draw further attention to how Shakespeare has crafted *Measure for Measure* and the subtle ways in which he weaves together dramatic devices, structure, plot, form and language into a cohesive whole.

You need to develop your own interpretation of the play and be able to express this confidently, supporting your argument with evidence and taking account of the historical, social and cultural context in which it was written. You also need to be aware of how the play has been received and re-interpreted over time.

The 'Key skills' boxes and the section on 'Boosting your skills' address the demands of the Assessment Objectives which underpin the examination across all examination boards and will help you to write fluent, well-structured academic essays which take account of the examination board criteria.

Do not feel that you have to attempt all the activities in the workbook: select according to your needs. However, there is a progression within each section, from the basics in 'Starting out' through 'Developing your ideas' to the more challenging 'Taking it further' activities. Take note of the key terms boxes to widen your critical vocabulary and try tackling the 'Challenge yourself' boxes if your aim is to achieve the top grades.

Measure for Measure is a play that repays advanced study: it is as timely and resonant in the early decades of the twenty-first century as it was at the beginning of the seventeenth century.

Line and scene references are to the updated Cambridge edition of *Measure for Measure* edited by Brian Gibbons (Cambridge University Press, 2012).

Plot and dramatic structure

What happens when and where is the basis of the plot of *Measure for Measure*. It is important to demonstrate that you have a detailed knowledge of the plot and an understanding of why Shakespeare chose to have things happen in this way and in this order.

Shakespeare's sources

Shakespeare's originality lay in the way he handled and developed existing plots rather than in creating new stories. The sources for *Measure for Measure* include a tale by the sixteenth-century Italian writer Cinthio and an English play by George Whetstone, based on that tale and performed in 1578. That play, *Promos and Cassandra*, has definite plot similarities with *Measure for Measure* but Shakespeare's version is richer and subtler in its exploration of the ideas of justice and morality.

1 (a) Fill in the table below to show how the major source, *Promos and Cassandra*, compares with *Measure for Measure*. Circle the score you think is appropriate: the greater the similarity between the two plays, the higher the score.

The city of Julio is Vienna for Shakespeare and the characters' names are: Andrugio/Claudio; Cassandra/Isabella; Promos/Angelo.

OUTLINE OF *PROMOS AND CASSANDRA*	HOW SIMILAR IS *MEASURE FOR MEASURE?*
A Promos is appointed by the king to rule over the city of Julio.	Different Similar 1 2 3 4 5 6 7 8 9 10
B There are low-life characters involved in selling sex.	Different Similar 1 2 3 4 5 6 7 8 9 10
C Promos sentences Andrugio to death for lechery.	Different Similar 1 2 3 4 5 6 7 8 9 10
D Andrugio appeals to his sister Cassandra to plead with Promos.	Different Similar 1 2 3 4 5 6 7 8 9 10
E Cassandra meets Promos, who delays the execution.	Different Similar 1 2 3 4 5 6 7 8 9 10
F Promos reveals in a soliloquy that he is unable to subdue his desire for Cassandra.	Different Similar 1 2 3 4 5 6 7 8 9 10
G When Cassandra meets Promos again, he makes his indecent proposal. Horrified, she refuses.	Different Similar 1 2 3 4 5 6 7 8 9 10
H Cassandra tells her brother of Promos's vile proposal and tries to prepare him for death.	Different Similar 1 2 3 4 5 6 7 8 9 10
I Andrugio appeals to his sister to accept Promos's proposal and save his life.	Different Similar 1 2 3 4 5 6 7 8 9 10
J Brother and sister argue, but finally Cassandra agrees to go to Promos.	Different Similar 1 2 3 4 5 6 7 8 9 10

CONTINUED ➔

K	After satisfying his desire, Promos breaks his word, believing that Cassandra will not reveal her own shame.	Different									Similar
		1	2	3	4	5	6	7	8	9	10
L	Andrugio is secretly freed by the jailer and goes into hiding.	Different									Similar
		1	2	3	4	5	6	7	8	9	10
M	Promos orders that Andrugio should be executed and his head sent to Cassandra. (A substitute head is sent.)	Different									Similar
		1	2	3	4	5	6	7	8	9	10
N	Promos is punished by the king on his return. He has to marry Cassandra before being executed. She pleads for him to be spared.	Different									Similar
		1	2	3	4	5	6	7	8	9	10
O	Andrugio returns. He is reunited with Cassandra and Promos is pardoned.	Different									Similar
		1	2	3	4	5	6	7	8	9	10

(b) Shakespeare made the following changes from his most obvious source, *Promos and Cassandra*:
- He expanded the Duke's role by having him disguised as a friar.
- He made Isabella a novice, not just a young woman.
- He introduced Lucio, who moves between social classes.
- He expanded the 'low-life' dimension.
- He introduced the 'bed trick' with Mariana to preserve Isabella's virtue.
- He had the Duke invite Isabella to marry him.

Decide which of the points above you think is the most significant and using the template below, write a paragraph on Shakespeare's use of his main source, *Promos and Cassandra*, providing supporting detail from the play.

Shakespeare increased the dramatic impact of 'Measure for Measure' by adapting his main source. The most significant example of this is ....

....

....

....

This enabled Shakespeare to ....

....

....

....

....

KEY SKILLS

Examiners never want you to simply retell the plot of the play. They want you to use your knowledge of the play to answer the question set. For example, you could comment on how and why Shakespeare's plot differs from that of his main source as part of your exploration of his dramatic craft.

2   Look through the list below and use these events, actual and anticipated, to complete the table showing what does (and does not) happen:

- Lucio marries Kate Keepdown
- Angelo is executed
- Claudio makes Julietta pregnant
- Pompey is executed
- Angelo marries Mariana
- The Duke marries Isabella
- Lucio is executed
- Angelo abandons Mariana
- Barnadine is executed
- Vienna descends into depravity
- Claudio is executed
- Isabella is propositioned by Angelo
- Claudio pleads for his life
- Isabella decides to become a nun
- The Duke recognises his own laxity

EVENTS THAT HAPPENED BEFORE THE PLAY	EVENTS THAT HAPPEN DURING THE PLAY	ANTICIPATED EVENTS THAT DO NOT HAPPEN

3   Check your knowledge of the play by answering these questions.

(a) Whose advice does Duke Vincentio seek over Angelo's suitability to deputise for him?

....

(b) Which contemporary figure could be alluded to when the Duke says, 'I love the people, / But do not like to stage me to their eyes.'

....

(c) Who is the dramatic link between the 'low-life' characters and the nobility?

....

(d) What explanation does the Duke give to Friar Thomas for leaving Angelo in charge of Vienna?

....

CONTINUED ➡

(e) What does Angelo say, when talking to Escalus in Act 2 Scene 1, that prepares the audience for what will happen later in the play?

....

(f) How does Mariana enable Isabel to remain a virgin?

....

(g) Whose head is substituted for Claudio's?

....

(h) What justification does the Duke give for making Isabella believe that her brother has been executed?

....

(i) How does Shakespeare create dramatic tension around the return of the Duke?

....

(j) What provides evidence of Isabella's Christian goodness in the final scene?

....

KEY SKILLS

Embedding textual references

When building an argument, try to clinch your points by including relevant textual details within the flow of your sentences. For example, when analysing the play's structure, you might write: 'Shakespeare signalled to the audience early on that Angelo would prove false by having him declare that, "When I that censure him do so offend, / Let mine own judgement pattern out my death." (2.1.30–1).'

DEVELOPING YOUR IDEAS

Measure for Measure does not fit neatly within the conventions of either tragedy or comedy. It has been called a 'problem play' by many critics. The denouement, where marriage rather than murder is the culmination of the play, is very much in line with comic convention yet its impact is not comfortably comic.

4   Look at the following 15 episodes and decide whether you think they are closer to tragedy or comedy. Bear in mind the definitions of tragedy and comedy on page 6 as you decide.

A   The Duke hands over to Angelo the power of life and death in Vienna (1.1).

B   Claudio is arrested for fornication (1.2).

C   Isabella is persuaded to plead for Claudio's life (1.4).

D   Pompey is arrested by Elbow for being a bawd (2.1).

E   Isabella's pleading with Angelo awakens his desire for her (2.2).

F   Angelo tells Isabella that her virginity is the price for Claudio's pardon (2.4).

G   Claudio begs Isabella to sacrifice herself to save his life (3.1).

H   Pompey is imprisoned and Lucio refuses to stand bail for him (3.2).

I   Persuaded by the Duke, Mariana agrees to 'the bed trick' (4.1).

J   Angelo goes back on his promise to save Claudio but the Duke persuades the Provost to substitute Barnadine's head for Claudio's (4.2).

K   Barnardine proves hard to catch and kill, but the pirate Ragozine's head is conveniently available (4.3).

CONTINUED

L The Duke plans his return to the city and prepares Isabella to denounce Angelo (4.5 and 6).

M The Duke returns and pretends to believe Angelo (5.1).

N Angelo's conduct is revealed and condemned, but Mariana and Isabella plead for his life (5.1).

O Claudio is revealed to be alive, Angelo (and Lucio) are pardoned but (like Isabella) are ordered to marry (5.1).

(a) Use the table below to record your responses. Fill in the appropriate square for each episode using the sidebar numbering to record your judgement with emojis – a sad face for tragic and a happy face for comic. The higher the number the greater the degree of comic or tragic impact of the episode as shown for episodes A–D in the example below.

It was one student's view that episode A, the Duke's disappearance, had tragic potential, so she rated it as 2 on the scale for tragic impact. For episode B, Claudio's arrest, she felt that the tragic potential was obvious and rated it as 8. Episode C, Isabella's pleading, she rated as 7 because there was still hope for Claudio. For episode D, where Elbow enters, her rating was a high 9 for comic.

You may disagree with the student's example. If so, make your own entries for episodes A–D before completing the rest of the chart. For some episodes you may want to indicate a mixture of comic and tragic.

TRAGIC OR COMIC?

	A	B	C	D	E	F	G	H	I	J	K	L	M	N	O
10															
9				☺											
8		☹													
7			☹												
6															
5															
4															
3															
2	☹														
1															
EPISODES	A	B	C	D	E	F	G	H	I	J	K	L	M	N	O

(b) Create an image of your reaction to the play in terms of its tragic and comic elements by joining up your emojis with one line for tragic and a separate line for comic. Use different colours for each line.

Tragedy: A drama or literary work in which the main character suffers and (in Shakespeare) dies because of a tragic flaw or moral weakness.

Comedy: An amusing play, often satirical in tone, that has a cheerful ending. It features triumph over adversity, often through disguise or deception, by creating comic characters and situations.

Denouement: In drama the denouement is the final outcome, generally occurring after the climax of the plot. It is where the strands of the plot are drawn together and matters are explained or resolved.

CONTINUED ➡

5   What picture of the play emerges from your charting of tragic and comic? Were there episodes that were neither tragic nor comic, or episodes that had elements of both?

Use your findings to complete the following:

The parts of the play that are predominantly tragic are ....

....

....

....

The parts of the play that are predominantly comic are ....

....

....

Although it was classified as a comedy on first publication, many critics have seen *Measure for Measure* as a tragicomedy, combining elements of tragic and comic. This may be reflected in your chart.

Challenge yourself

In 1987 the critic Gregory Lanier wrote of *Measure for Measure* that there is 'a juxtaposition of two dramatic modes, tragedy and comedy, carefully poised to create a cohesive, resonant unity'. To what extent do you agree with Lanier's claim?

Time in *Measure for Measure*

Dramatic time is not the same as conventional time. In *Measure for Measure,* as J. W. Lever, editor of the Arden edition, suggested, the timescale is slippery: the speed at which the tragic plot develops contrasts with the deliberately slow-paced comic development. Things seem simultaneously to have been happening over a long period (for example, the Duke's absence or Pompey's reoffending) and yet happen very quickly as the time for Claudio's execution nears.

6   What do you notice about:

(a) the duration of the Duke's absence

....

....

(b) the different times set for Claudio's execution

....

....

(c) the time Pompey and Mistress Overdone have been running a 'hot-house'

....

....

(d) the length of time the Friar has been Mariana's counsellor?

....

....

CONTINUED ➔

Answers can be found at: www.hoddereducation.co.uk/workbookanswers

7   To what extent do you agree with the view of Cedric Watts that 'we concentrate in the play on "human interest" rather than on details of clock-time or calendar time'?

....

....

Challenge yourself

Using the internet or J. W. Lever's Arden edition of *Measure for Measure* (pp. 14–15), find out how the story of 'The Disguised Ruler' featured in Elizabethan writing of the 1580s. Explore its relevance to *Measure for Measure*.

The social scales

The moral complexity of *Measure for Measure* is contributed to by the play of ideas across the social strata. What happens higher up the social scale with regard to sex before marriage is paralleled, illuminated and satirised by what happens at lower social levels.

8   List the main characters involved in three issues which are explored at different social levels. The first has been done for you:

ISSUE	HIGHER	MIDDLE	LOWER
Sex and/or marriage	Angelo, the Duke	Isabella, Mariana, Claudio, Julietta	Lucio and Kate Keepdown; Pompey and Mistress Overdone
Honesty and lies			
Justice and mercy			

KEY SKILLS

Analysing structure

Demonstrate your understanding of how the structure of *Measure for Measure* contributes to and influences our response to the play as a whole, especially its ideas. For example, how is an audience's view of marriage influenced by the fact that although Lucio and Angelo differ in character, attitude and social rank, both finally compelled to marry a woman they have wronged.

9 It has been suggested that the low characters do not constitute a minor plot, rather that they provide an alternative, careless and almost carnival-like contrast with the main plot. In this view their chief role is to provide comic relief from the tragedy, for while the play is a comedy, much of its action is tragic in nature. Complete the table below with evidence for and against this claim. The first row has been done for you.

THE CHIEF ROLE OF THE LOW CHARACTERS IS TO PROVIDE COMIC RELIEF	THE LOW CHARACTERS CONTRIBUTE MORE THAN COMIC RELIEF
(a) They do not directly influence what happens to the main characters.	(a) They provide a commentary on what is happening in the higher ranks of society.
(b)	(b)
(c)	(c)

Challenge yourself

Look at the final scenes of Shakespeare's *Othello,* indisputably a tragedy, and *Much Ado About Nothing*, very much a comedy, and identify points of similarity and/or contrast with *Measure for Measure*.

Challenge yourself

In 1599 King James I wrote a book of instructions on kingship for his son Henry. It was called *Basilikon Doron*. Parts of *Measure for Measure* are similar to James's words and ideas. Carry out your own research into James's ideas on the role and duties of a ruler and decide how much of James can be seen in the Duke, remembering that Shakespeare would have known that his patron King James would see the play's first performance.

TAKING IT FURTHER

A play is not accidental: it is a dramatic construct, shaped by the writer in deliberate ways. It could be argued that *Measure for Measure* is a play of ideas and emotions rather than of action because not much action takes place within the timeframe of the play itself.

10 Below are several comments on the structure of *Measure for Measure*. Think carefully about each one and decide how convincing you think it is. Give each a score out of 10 (10 = completely convincing).

COMMENT ON THE STRUCTURE	DO YOU AGREE?
Only right at the end, in the last hundred lines, does the play turn into a comedy.	/10
Measure for Measure is a play of powerful arguments and big ideas rather than action.	/10
Measure for Measure is a strange mixture of a play which juxtaposes scabrous humour with moral exploration.	/10
Measure for Measure is a play that asks big questions but they are not answered through its convenient and conventionally comic conclusion.	/10

CONTINUED ➡

Answers can be found at: www.hoddereducation.co.uk/workbookanswers

Measure for Measure is a play of two halves, and the first half is far more interesting than the second.	/10
The Duke is in control of the play throughout, stage-managing the other characters on Shakespeare's behalf.	/10
In *Measure for Measure* what happens to the female characters never seems to matter as much as what happens to the male characters.	/10

11 Now look at the perspective you found the most convincing. Using the template below, write a paragraph on the dramatic structure of *Measure for Measure*.

The most convincing argument is that the structure of 'Measure for Measure' is [summarise the perspective in your own words] ....

....

....

Nevertheless, a different view is possible because [provide supporting details from the play] .....

....

....

My personal opinion is that ....

....

....

KEY SKILLS

Supporting your argument

You should always support your argument – even if it based on a recognised critical perspective – through detailed references to the play.

Challenge yourself

Give yourself 15 minutes to plan and up to one hour to write the essay below.
'The Duke's is a fantastically orderly ending for a fantastically disorderly play.' (Everett 2003)
How far do you agree with this view of the ending of *Measure for Measure*?

Themes

Themes are major ideas that a writer presents and explores through a text. In *Measure for Measure* many of the themes are developed through imagery or balanced oppositions such as justice and mercy; good and bad government; life and death; purity and promiscuity; men and women; law and liberty and appearance and reality.

STARTING OUT

1 Below are some of the critically recognised themes in *Measure for Measure*. (Remember, however, that themes are not definitive: different interpretations might emphasise different themes.) Complete this table by adding what you think are three key dramatic moments in the play which feature or focus on each of these themes. The first has been done as an example.

THEME	THREE KEY DRAMATIC MOMENTS
A Good and bad government	1 The Duke handing his 'terror' to Angelo 2 Angelo exploiting his power to try to seduce Isabella 3 The Friar using the Duke's authority to save Claudio's life
B Justice and mercy	
C Life and death	
D Purity and promiscuity	
E Men and women	
F Law and liberty	
G Appearance and reality	

KEY SKILLS

Always remember that *Measure for Measure* was written for the stage, not the page. When writing about a particular scene or phrase, try to visualise the impact it might have had on a seventeenth-century audience in the royal court or Shakespeare's Globe. Then consider how a modern audience might see issues (notably the role of women) differently.

DEVELOPING YOUR IDEAS

2   Look at the statements about *Measure for Measure* in the table below. Circle your reaction to each statement in the second column and then use the remaining columns to provide textual evidence and analysis that explore your reaction. Again the first has been done as an example.

STATEMENT	DO YOU AGREE?	TEXTUAL EVIDENCE	YOUR ANALYSIS
A The most important theme is that of justice and mercy.	DEFINITELY PROBABLY (POSSIBLY) CERTAINLY NOT	ANGELO: What's open made to justice, That justice seizes. (2.1.20–21) ESCALUS: Mercy is not itself, that oft looks so (2.1.245) ISABELLA: No ceremony that to great ones longs, … Become them with one half so good a grace As mercy does. (2.2.60–64) ISABELLA: … lawful mercy Is nothing kin to foul redemption. (2.4.113–14) ISABELLA: … justice, justice, justice, justice! (5.1.25) DUKE: The very mercy of the law cries out … 'An Angelo for Claudio, death for death!' (5.1.400–403) DUKE: Like doth quit like, and measure still for measure. (5.1.404) ANGELO: … I crave death more willingly than mercy; (5.1.468)	This is not necessarily the most important theme, but it is certainly a major one. The play is framed around judgement and weighing justice against mercy (hence its title). As Escalus points out, mercy may not be merciful in its consequences, but the Duke's experience suggests that justice without mercy is destructive. At the ending he is merciful to (nearly) all. There is sustained focus on judging the character of those who administer the law, as well as those who break the law and a recognition that to err is to be human.

CONTINUED ➔

11

B	The play is essentially about sexual relationships.	DEFINITELY PROBABLY POSSIBLY CERTAINLY NOT		
C	The play's central theme is how to be a good ruler.	DEFINITELY PROBABLY POSSIBLY CERTAINLY NOT		
D	The deeper meanings of the play are about life and death.	DEFINITELY PROBABLY POSSIBLY CERTAINLY NOT		
E	A major theme is that purity should be avoided as much as promiscuity.	DEFINITELY PROBABLY POSSIBLY CERTAINLY NOT		
F	The play's main idea is that without law there can be no true liberty.	DEFINITELY PROBABLY POSSIBLY CERTAINLY NOT		

CONTINUED ➡

Answers can be found at: www.hoddereducation.co.uk/workbookanswers

G	The exploration of appearance and reality is a central theme in this as in other Shakespeare plays.	DEFINITELY PROBABLY POSSIBLY CERTAINLY NOT		

KEY SKILLS

Pay deliberate attention to the key words and images that echo through *Measure for Measure*. Key words include justice, mercy, liberty, law, pardon, chastity, death, life, love, sense and seeming. Major patterns of imagery include clothing, coinage, horse riding and a range of sexual images and innuendo. Be ready to comment on what these words and images might have meant to Shakespeare's audiences as well as to modern audiences.

TAKING IT FURTHER

3   Consider the extracts (A-G) below, from student essays on different themes. Choose two or three of these extracts and annotate them as shown in the example:

(a) Identify four positive qualities in the extract.

(b) Find three relevant quotations which would improve the extract by giving textual evidence for the points made and show where they could be added.

(A) GOOD AND BAD GOVERNMENT

The theme of good and bad government is explored primarily through the contrast between Angelo and the Duke. Angelo, who uses public powers for his private ends, is exposed as a hypocrite while the Duke (modelled in part on James I) observes, manipulates and marries off the characters for the general good (i).

The ruler-in-disguise stratagem would have been familiar to Shakespeare's audience and it enables Duke Vincentio (like Severus in classical tales) to learn about good government while incognito (ii). Shakespeare adds a human (and humorous) twist by having the Duke react so personally to Lucio's baiting (a). The Duke, as he admits at the start of the play, has much to regret about his rule, and by using the 'disguised ruler' strategy of folk tale he comes to a deeper understanding that simplistic approaches such as the severity of Angelo do not fit comfortably with flawed human nature. There are references to kingly qualities that James I would have admired (iii) (b), but at times the Duke (like Prospero) resembles a stage manager struggling to manipulate his characters and to arrange the performance he has planned.

CONTINUED ➡

Angelo, whose use of public power to pursue his private lust is what rulers should avoid, compares the Duke to power divine but his lack of power when disguised reduces him to hastily invented stratagems to preserve Claudio's life and exposes him to Lucio's disconcerting vituperation (iv) (c). His claim to have avoided 'the dribbling dart of love' is exposed as self-delusion when, one sign of his humanity, he marries Isabella.

Positives:

(i) clear line of argument established early on

(ii) informed comment on sources

(iii) awareness of contemporary historical context

(iv) economy of phrasing.

Quotations:

(a) DUKE: No might nor greatness in mortality / Can censure 'scape (3.2.158–9)

(b) ESCALUS: One that, above all other strifes, contended especially to know himself. (3.2.199)
   ESCALUS: … a gentleman of all temperance. (3.2.201)

(c) ANGELO: … your grace, like power divine, / Hath look'd upon my passes. (5.1.362–3)

(B) JUSTICE AND MERCY

The lasting impact of 'Measure for Measure' is the feeling that mercy is more powerful than justice because we are all too flawed to judge each other. The play is an intellectual and dramatic exploration of what justice is and is not, framed within the conventions of a comedy. We are shown an image of powerful injustice in Angelo, whose attempt to separate the judge from the judgement is shown as hypocrisy, and yet everyone is pardoned at the end of the play. The message that to err is human, and that forgiveness is possible, is closer to the New Testament than the 'like doth quit like' approach of the Old Testament.

Isabella needs to be prompted by Lucio before she can find the eloquence to advocate mercy and she herself is not merciful to her brother Claudio when her chastity is at stake. A vocal central character in the first half of the play, increasingly powerful in her pleading to Angelo, Isabella becomes a silenced figure in the final scene. Within the play as a whole mercy wins out in the end, matching Isabella's earlier evocation of its appropriateness, but her own commitment to mercy is left open to question, more likely to be resolved by a director's interpretation than by Shakespeare's enigmatic presentation of Isabella's character.

Positives:

(i) ....

(ii) ....

CONTINUED

(iii) ....

(iv) ....

Quotations:

(a) ....

(b) ....

(c) ....

(C) LIFE AND DEATH

The play begins with punishment for an impending birth and ends with the avoidance of expected deaths. In between, death is an ever-present element in the conversations, especially since 'to die' was an Elizabethan term for having sex. Many of the characters face death at some point, or like Isabella talk about why they might prefer death to shameful life. Claudio's evocation of fear of death is one of the most powerful speeches in Shakespeare, put in the mouth of a character whose ordinariness is his most notable feature. His oscillation in choosing between a shameful life and a fearful death is one of the most dramatic moments of the play, but the audience is soon aware that the Duke will not allow him to die. We therefore look on his preparedness for death with more distanced eyes.

Comic convention requires that the play ends with marriages rather than murders, but as Lucio laments, the two are not always clearly distinguishable. The exploration of life and death in the earlier part of the play has tragic intensity but is diminished in the later part by the comic conventions requiring betrothals not beheadings.

Positives:

(i) ....

(ii) ....

(iii) ....

(iv) ....

Quotations:

(a) ....

(b) ....

(c) ....

(D) PURITY AND PROMISCUITY

Nowhere in the play do we see a balance between purity and promiscuity: all we see is a choice between the two. Angelo's corrupt hypocrisy is more

CONTINUED →

likely to undermine the integrity and well-being of Vienna's society than the casual immorality of Pompey and Mistress Overdone. It is presented dramatically as much more significant and may well reflect Shakespeare's view on the puritanical tendency that was seeking to close down theatres as part of its crusade against sexual licence.

Chastity was a pearl of great price in Shakespeare's day when inheritance could depend on the purity of a family bloodline. Daughters were expected to remain chaste and obey their fathers, and wives to be faithful to their husbands. In 'Measure for Measure' there is an untypical absence of fathers so both Isabella and Mariana are free to take decisions about their own lives. Isabella embodies chastity and innocence, yet her purity fans the flames of Angelo's desire and puts her at risk of rape. Mariana is ready to lose her chastity and reputation to regain Angelo. When the Duke announces that Isabella is to marry him, audiences make what they will of her significant silence. We never know how Kate Keepdown feels at the prospect of Lucio.

Positives:

(i) ....

(ii) ....

(iii) ....

(iv) ....

Quotations:

(a) ....

(b) ....

(c) ....

(E) MEN AND WOMEN

This is a play of ideas and argument rather than action. It is built around reflection on, rather than experience of, sexual relationships. Sex is talked of incessantly and features throughout in the imagery, even (or especially) in Isabella's declaration that she will 'strip herself to death, as to a bed', but physical love is never shown in the way it is in 'Antony and Cleopatra'.

The position of women in Shakespeare's time was usually determined by men, Queen Elizabeth I being a notable exception. Men are the dominant figures in terms of physical and social power: women are expected to withdraw (to a nunnery or moated grange) rather than to offer open opposition. Nevertheless, the dominance of Angelo is shown to be corrupt and his desires are thwarted by the subtler, female-focused strategies of the Duke.

CONTINUED

Answers can be found at: www.hoddereducation.co.uk/workbookanswers

It is the women who ultimately triumph, except perhaps for Isabella, since Mariana and Kate Keepdown achieve the marriages they desire. There are times when women's socially determined helplessness is dramatically more powerful than official power structures: the image of Mariana has the 'soft power' of the romantic imagination. Modern audiences are more likely than a seventeenth-century audience to be aware of the roles women are expected/allowed to occupy and to feel that 'Measure for Measure' is about the abuse of women not just about the abuse of power.

Positives:

(i) ....

(ii) ....

(iii) ....

(iv) ....

Quotations:

(a) ....

(b) ....

(c) ....

(F) LAW AND LIBERTY

The play is in part an exploration of what justice is, and in part an illumination of the way justice is administered. The official defenders of the faith in justice are shown to be lacking – Elbow's inadequacy is shown through his 'misplacings' of language and Escalus asks a key question about 'justice or iniquity' to which Shakespeare never gives a definitive answer. When Pompey moves from being 'an unlawful bawd' to being a 'lawful hangman' the irony is not lost upon the audience. Angelo's corruption raises questions about whether those administering the law need to be virtuous for a law to be valid in its application.

One of the play's key questions is about the balance between liberty and restraint. The initial image of a decadent Vienna suggests that liberty, if unrestrained, causes problems. Isabella initially seeks the total restraint of St Clare's, yet finishes with the different restraint that marriage brings. The low-lifers embody freedom from restraints yet are punished more by disease than by the law. As Pompey points out, the decisions as to what is or is not lawful are slippery in that legal killing may be a worse crime than unlawful lechery. Our moral guides, in addition to the Duke, are the Provost and Escalus but 'Measure for Measure' is a play which tries, and fails, to identify an appropriate balance between law and liberty.

CONTINUED

Positives:

(i) ....

(ii) ....

(iii)...

(iv) ....

Quotations:

(a) ....

(b) ....

(c) ....

(G) APPEARANCE AND REALITY

At the heart of what Shakespeare calls 'seeming' is the hypocrisy of power, and the play's messages about such hypocrisy matter to today's audiences as much as to the original audience. 'Measure for Measure', like the art of theatre, uses illusion (deceit) to conceal and reveal truths. Angelo's deceit is exposed through the Duke's deceitful stratagems, making it difficult for any audience to claim that deception is, or is not, wrong.

The Duke uses some of the techniques featured in Machiavelli's cynical guide to princes on how to obtain and retain power. Despite what some critics have claimed, Duke Vincentio is not presented as an omniscient, omnipotent God-like being: he is presented as a man who has partial understanding of himself and others. He is reduced to hasty subterfuge to bring about his desired outcomes and takes decisions (such as substituting Mariana for Isabella) that many of his contemporaries could have seen as morally problematic.

Positives:

(i) ....

(ii) ....

(iii)...

(iv)...

Quotations:

(a) ....

(b) ....

(c) ....

CONTINUED ➜

Answers can be found at: www.hoddereducation.co.uk/workbookanswers

4   Shakespeare did not write themes – he wrote plays in which themes contribute to the dramatic impact. The themes in *Measure for Measure* are not independent of each other, so having considered themes separately it is important to explore ways in which they relate to and illuminate each other.

Create a spider diagram for each of the quotations (a)–(e) below illustrating which themes you think are relevant to that quotation and explaining the significance of the quotation for each theme you identify. The first has been done as an example.

(a)   DUKE: … hence shall we see, / If power change purpose, what our seemers be. **(1.3.54–5)**

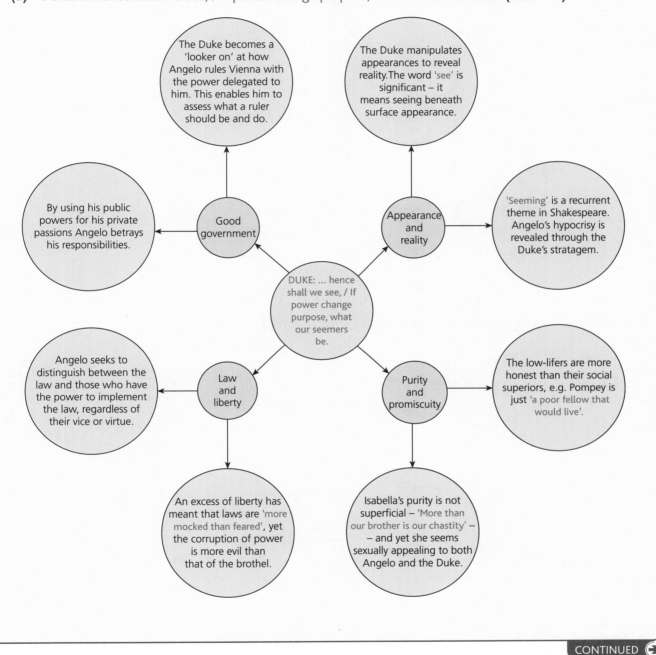

CONTINUED ➡

(b) ESCALUS: Which is the wiser here? Justice or Iniquity? **(2.1.148)**

(c) ISABELLA: More than our brother is our chastity. **(2.4.186)**

CONTINUED

Answers can be found at: www.hoddereducation.co.uk/workbookanswers

(d) CLAUDIO: To sue to live, I find I seek to die; / And, seeking death, find life: let it come on. **(3.1.43–4)**

(e) ESCALUS: One that, above all other strifes, contended especially to know himself. **(3.2.199)**

CONTINUED ➡

5   Look again at the final scene of *Measure for Measure*. Write a paragraph on how successful you think it is in providing a dramatic resolution for the thematic issues presented during the play.

....

....

....

....

....

....

....

....

....

....

KEY SKILLS

Focusing on an extract

Even if the exam question asks you to look at the play as a whole, it can be useful to spend **some** time in your response focusing on a particular passage. This will help you to demonstrate a detailed appreciation of Shakespeare's crafting of the play, as well as specific awareness of how relationships and ideas are developed within the passage.

Challenge yourself

Read or watch the first two scenes of Shakespeare's last play *The Tempest*. Identify ways in which Prospero's account of his time ruling Milan relates to and differs from the Duke's situation in Vienna.

Characterisation

Always remember that characters in a drama are not people: they are an author's **constructs**. The characters created by Shakespeare in *Measure for Measure* have dramatic roles rather than individual destinies.

Construct: A character created by an author for his dramatic purposes as opposed to a 'real' person.

STARTING OUT

1   Match the characters listed below with their quotations and say in what ways the quotation is or is not typical of that character. The first one has been done for you.

- Isabella
- The Duke
- Angelo
- Lucio

- Claudio
- Escalus
- Pompey
- Elbow

QUOTATION	CHARACTER	TYPICAL OR NOT?
A ... for your lovely sake Give me your hand, and say you will be mine (5.1.484–5)	Duke	Untypical in that the Duke claimed to be immune to 'the dribbling dart of love', yet here declares his wish to marry Isabella.
B Your sense pursues not mine: either you are ignorant Or seem so crafty, and that's not good. (2.4.74–5)		
C I hold you as a thing enskied and sainted, By your renouncement an immortal spirit, And to be talked with in sincerity As with a saint. (1.4.34–7)		
D Which is the wiser here, Justice or Iniquity? (2.1.148)		
E ... thou art to continue, now, thou varlet; thou art to continue. (2.1.162–3)		
F The weariest and most loathéd worldly life That age, ache, penury, and imprisonment Can lay on nature, is a paradise To what we fear of death. (3.1.129–32)		

CONTINUED ➔

G	Truly, sir, I am a poor fellow that would live. (2.1.191)		
H	Is't not a kind of incest to take life From thine own sister's shame? (3.1.139–40)		

KEY SKILLS

Avoid writing about characters as though they were real people. Demonstrate to the examiner that you are aware that they are constructs by using expressions like 'shown to be', 'presented as', 'constructed as' and 'created to'.

DEVELOPING YOUR IDEAS

Coins, coinage and coining are recurrent images in the play. Like coins, most of the characters (apart from Escalus and the low-life ones) have two distinct sides, can be tested for their mettle/metal and may or may not ring true. The most obvious example is the Duke, who has two 'faces', as ruler and as friar.

2   Complete the (a)–(d) boxes below with textual evidence to show how the characters listed could be said to have at least two sides to their dramatic characters and add your own comment. The first has been done as an example.

(a)   The Duke

RULER	FRIAR

DUKE: … we have with special soul / Elected him
  our absence to supply,
  Lent him our terror, dressed him with our love
 (1.1.17–19)
	DUKE: … a purpose
	  More grave and wrinkled than the aims and ends
	  Of burning youth.
	 (1.3.4–6)

DUKE: … I love the people, But do not like to stage me to their eyes (1.1.67–8)	DUKE: I am confessor to Angelo (3.1.164)
DUKE: … for this fourteen years we have let slip (1.3.23)	DUKE: … the love I have in doing good (3.1.191)

DUKE: Sith 'twas my fault to give the people scope,
  'Twould be my tyranny to strike and gall them
  For what I bid them do
 (1.3.36–8)
	DUKE: … the doubleness of the benefit defends
	  the deceit from reproof
	 (3.1.240–41)

DUKE: We shall see,
  If power change purpose, what our seemers be.
 (1.3.54–5)
	DUKE: I never heard the absent Duke much
	  detected for women; he was not inclin'd
	  that way.
	 (3.2.105–7)

	DUKE: … he shall appear to the envious a scholar, a statesman and a soldier. (3.2.125)

CONTINUED

COMMENT
- The Duke's double identity, as ruler and as friar, is a source of entertainment for the audience as well as a dramatic mechanism for allowing him to transfer his learning between his two identities.
- This dual personality means the Duke can participate in the action while being removed from it.
- As both friar and ruler, Vincentio combines the power of Church and state, spiritual and secular.
- In exposing Angelo and marrying Isabella, Vincentio acts as a ruler on the basis of what he has learnt as a friar.

(b) Isabella

PURE SAINT	PASSIONATE SEXUAL BEING

COMMENT

(c) Angelo

'PRECISE' PURITAN	LUSTFUL HYPOCRITE

CONTINUED ➡

COMMENT

(d) Claudio

COURAGE	COWARDICE

COMMENT

KEY SKILLS

Historical and cultural context

You should demonstrate in your responses an understanding of how Shakespeare's historical and cultural context influenced the conception and development of his characters. For example, the portrayal of Angelo's puritanical severity might well have reflected Shakespeare's attitude to the puritans who were seeking to close down the London theatres on which his living depended.

Isabella and Mariana

3   Isabella and Mariana differ in situation and character, yet there are similarities between them. Complete the table below identifying the degree of some of those similarities and differences by circling a score out of 10. The higher the number, the greater the similarity.

ASPECT	HOW SIMILAR ARE ISABELLA AND MARIANA?
Trusts the Friar	Different Similar 1 2 3 4 5 6 7 8 9 10
Believes in the importance of chastity	Different Similar 1 2 3 4 5 6 7 8 9 10
Argues articulately	Different Similar 1 2 3 4 5 6 7 8 9 10
Marries according to the Duke's wish	Different Similar 1 2 3 4 5 6 7 8 9 10
Is subject to the power of men	Different Similar 1 2 3 4 5 6 7 8 9 10
Does what she believes is right	Different Similar 1 2 3 4 5 6 7 8 9 10
Accepts that deception can be justified	Different Similar 1 2 3 4 5 6 7 8 9 10
Is betrayed by Angelo	Different Similar 1 2 3 4 5 6 7 8 9 10
Wishes to remain chaste	Different Similar 1 2 3 4 5 6 7 8 9 10

4   In the final scene Isabella is noticeably silent when the Duke claims her hand in marriage. Write below what you imagine Isabella thinks but does not say.

....

....

....

....

....

....

....

5   Write a paragraph confirming or challenging the view below:

> Shakespeare presents the female characters in *Measure for Measure* as women with the moral strength to expose the hypocrisy of male domination. (Remember that Isabella and Mariana are not the only female characters.)

....

....

....

CONTINUED ➔

....

....

....

....

....

6 Look at the statements about characters in *Measure for Measure* in the table below. Circle your reaction to each statement in the second column and then use the remaining columns to provide one or two key quotations and justify your reaction. The first has been done as an example.

STATEMENT	DO YOU AGREE?	KEY QUOTATIONS	YOUR JUSTIFICATION
A The Duke is not dramatically credible.	DEFINITELY (PROBABLY) POSSIBLY CERTAINLY NOT	ANGELO: ... your grace, like power divine, Hath looked upon my passes (5.1.362–3) DUKE: ... you may marvel why I obscured myself (5.1.383)	The Duke is created as a manipulator rather than a man. He is cruel to Isabella and while his betrothal to her could be seen as part of the humanising process he goes through, it strains audience belief.
B Isabella loses the sympathy of a modern audience.	DEFINITELY PROBABLY POSSIBLY CERTAINLY NOT		
C Claudio is too conventional for us to care about him.	DEFINITELY PROBABLY POSSIBLY CERTAINLY NOT		
D Lucio is the most appealing character in the play.	DEFINITELY PROBABLY POSSIBLY CERTAINLY NOT		

CONTINUED ➡

E	Pompey is more honest than those who condemn him.	DEFINITELY PROBABLY POSSIBLY CERTAINLY NOT		
F	Escalus is the only truly admirable character.	DEFINITELY PROBABLY POSSIBLY CERTAINLY NOT		
G	Mariana is simply pathetic.	DEFINITELY PROBABLY POSSIBLY CERTAINLY NOT		

Angelo and Isabella

7 (a) How does Shakespeare reveal the characters of Isabella and Angelo through the dialogue below? Annotate the extract paying particular attention to the use of pronouns and the movement of the verse.

> **ISABELLA**   Must he needs die?
>
> **ANGELO**   Maiden, no remedy.
>
> **ISABELLA**   Yes: I do think that you might pardon him,
> And neither heaven nor man grieve at the mercy.
>
> **ANGELO**   I will not do't.
>
> **ISABELLA**   But can you, if you would?
>
> **ANGELO**   Look, what I will not, that I cannot do.
>
> **ISABELLA**   But might you do't, and do the world no wrong,
> If so your heart were touched with that remorse
> As mine is to him?
>
> **ANGELO**   He's sentenced, 'tis too late.
> (2.2.48–57)

CONTINUED ➔

(b) Write a paragraph in which you explore the dramatic impact of this exchange.

....

....

....

....

....

....

....

....

....

The Duke

8   Below are various views on the Duke and other characters. Choose the comment that you find most interesting and write a brief paragraph about that comment using the frame provided.

   A   The Duke is an earlier version of Prospero in *The Tempest*, with the same power to manipulate other characters.

   B   The Duke's sensitivity to Lucio's carping comments make him a ridiculous figure in the eyes of the audience.

   C   The Duke is not a dramatically or psychologically convincing character. He is just created to fulfill the requirements of the plot.

   D   The Duke, with all his imperfections on his head, behaves more like a typical seventeenth-century ruler than an agent of divine providence.

   The view of the Duke that ....

   ....

   is supported by ....

   ....

   However ....

   ....

   My own interpretation is that ....

   ....

Isabella

9   Choose the comment below that is closest to your own view and write a justification for your choice.

   A   Isabella is like Angelo: she is an angel on the outside but with the devil within.

   B   Isabella is not just brighter than her brother, she has a spirituality that he cannot understand.

   C   Isabella cares more about ideals than about individuals, and that alienates a modern audience.

CONTINUED ➔

D   Isabella has to bear the burden of a powerful man's sexual misconduct and that gives her great appeal for a modern audience.

....

....

....

....

....

Claudio

10 Read the comments below and decide which you agree with most and which you agree with least. Write an explanation of the reasons behind your responses and provide the textual evidence on which those responses are based.

A   Claudio's oscillations are typical of a conventional young man. This is why audiences sympathise with him.

B   Shakespeare makes Claudio the only fully rounded character in the play with whom an audience can identify.

C   Claudio may be a bit feeble, but he does not deserve to be flayed by Isabella's fury and sent to death by her savage condemnation.

D   Claudio only comes to life dramatically when he is pleading for his life. Otherwise he is too ordinary to be interesting.

....

....

....

....

....

Angelo

11 Rate the comments below in terms of your agreement with them on a scale by circling 1–5. The higher the rating, the more you agree with the view expressed. Then write a brief explanation of your reactions on a separate sheet of paper, using your own words and supporting your points with quotations.

QUOTATION		RATING				
A	Angelo finds himself emotionally at sea because he is unfamiliar with human feeling.	1	2	3	4	5
B	Angelo's conduct may be despicable but his psychology is dramatically convincing and we agree with Isabella that sincerity did govern his actions initially.	1	2	3	4	5
C	Angelo is so confident of his abilities that he is bound to be the architect of his own downfall.	1	2	3	4	5
D	Angelo is a 'seemer', and the play's message is that all puritans are hypocritical like him.	1	2	3	4	5

CONTINUED ➔

Lucio

12 Choose the comment below that you find most interesting and write a brief paragraph about it using the frame provided or your preferred wording.

A Lucio is amusingly amoral, but his wit means that we, like the Duke, finally forgive him.

B Lucio has an important plot function because he is the link between the different levels of society.

C Audiences enjoy Lucio's baiting of the Duke and yet feel that it is justifiable to sentence him to marriage with Kate Keepdown.

D Lucio's refusal to rescue Pompey is the one time in the play when we part emotional company with him.

The view of Lucio that ....

....

is supported by ....

....

However ....

....

My own interpretation is that ....

....

TAKING IT FURTHER

Escalus and Pompey

13 Read and annotate the exchange below, underlining words which reveal the characters and attitudes of the speakers. Then, on a separate piece of paper, write a paragraph about the conversation in which you explain your response to the claim that:

When Escalus meets with Pompey the two worlds of Vienna collide on stage – the official world and the underworld.

ESCALUS ... Come you hither to me, Master Tapster. What's your name, Master Tapster?

POMPEY Pompey.

ESCALUS What else?

POMPEY Bum, sir.

ESCALUS Troth, and your bum is the greatest thing about you, so that in the beastliest sense you are Pompey the Great. Pompey, you are partly a bawd, Pompey, howsoever you colour it in being a tapster, are you not? Come, tell me true, it shall be the better for you.

CONTINUED

Answers can be found at: www.hoddereducation.co.uk/workbookanswers

POMPEY	Truly, sir, I am a poor fellow that would live.
ESCALUS	How would you live, Pompey? By being a bawd? What do you think of the trade, Pompey? Is it a lawful trade?
POMPEY	If the law would allow it, sir.
ESCALUS	But the law will not allow it, Pompey; nor it shall not be allowed in Vienna.
POMPEY	Does your worship mean to geld and splay all the youth of the city?
ESCALUS	No, Pompey.
POMPEY	Truly, sir, in my poor opinion, they will to't then. If your worship will take order for the drabs and the knaves, you need not to fear the bawds.
ESCALUS	There are pretty orders beginning, I can tell you: it is but heading and hanging.
POMPEY	If you head and hang all that offend that way but for ten year together, you'll be glad to give out a commission for more heads. If this law hold in Vienna ten year, I'll rent the fairest house in it after three pence a bay. If you live to see this come to pass, say Pompey told you so.
ESCALUS	Thank you, good Pompey; and, in requital of your prophecy, hark you: I advise you, let me not find you before me again upon any complaint whatsoever; no, not for dwelling where you do. If I do, Pompey, I shall beat you to your tent, and prove a shrewd Caesar to you: in plain dealing, Pompey, I shall have you whipped. So, for this time, Pompey, fare you well.
POMPEY	I thank your worship for your good counsel; [*Aside*] but I shall follow it as the flesh and fortune shall better determine.
	Whip me? No, no, let carman whip his jade,
	The valiant heart's not whipped out of his trade. [*Exit*]

(2.1.181–219)

Challenge yourself

Write a response in which you confirm, qualify or challenge the view stated below:

The play's characters are created by Shakespeare to illustrate particular human types which illuminate the main themes. For example, Isabella is a saintly virgin, Angelo a self-righteous puritan and Lucio a laughing libertine.

Writer's methods: Language and style

To achieve the grade you want you need to analyse the ways meanings are shaped in *Measure for Measure* through Shakespeare's choice and use of language.

STARTING OUT

Verse and prose

A quick flick through your copy of the play looking at line endings will give you a visual reminder that nearly two-thirds (62 per cent) is poetry and over a third (38 per cent) is prose.

1   Why did Shakespeare use verse at some times and prose at others? Look at the quotations below and, having identified whether they are verse or prose, identify the language features and analyse their dramatic impact. For example, you could look at the use of blank verse, alliteration, assonance, enjambement and caesura. The first has been done as an example.

	QUOTATION	VERSE OR PROSE?	LANGUAGE FEATURES AND DRAMATIC IMPACT
A	DUKE: ... Lord Angelo is precise, / Stands at a guard with envy, scarce confesses / That his blood flows, or that his appetite / Is more to bread than stone. Hence shall we see, / If power change purpose, what our seemers be. (1.3.51–5)	Verse	*This is formal verse from a high-status character. Enjambement allows the flow of sense from line to line. This allows Shakespeare to develop more elevated thoughts in the blank verse. The movement of the verse is balanced as the Duke reflects on Angelo's character. Here the final rhyming couplet signals the end of a scene.*
B	POMPEY: Sir, she came in great with child; and longing, saving your honour's reverence, for stewed prunes. Sir, we had but two in the house, which at that very distant time stood, as it were, in a fruit dish, a dish of some three pence; your honours have seen such dishes, they are not China dishes, but very good dishes – (2.1.81–5)		

CONTINUED ➔

C	ANGELO: ... What dost thou, or what art thou, Angelo? Dost thou desire her foully for those things That make her good? O, let her brother live: (2.2.177–9)		
D	DUKE: Shame to him whose cruel striking Kills for faults of his own liking. Twice treble shame on Angelo. To weed my vice and let his grow. (3.2.229–32)		

Avoid the trap of claiming that higher status characters invariably speak in blank verse: some characters, like the Duke or Lucio, use both verse and prose. In addition, at the end of Act 3 the Duke speaks in rhyming couplets.

Blank verse: The usual metre in Shakespeare is blank verse – blank meaning unrhymed, but there are times in *Measure for Measure* when rhymed verse is used. Blank verse is based on a line of ten syllables making five iambic feet, each with an unstressed (–) followed by a stressed (+) syllable as in the example below:

$$- \quad + \ / - \quad + \quad / - \quad + \quad / - \quad + \ / - \ +$$
We CAN/not WEIGH/ our BROTH/er WITH/ourSELF

Once this regular pattern has been established, Shakespeare varies it for dramatic purposes.

Alliteration: The repetition of a particular consonant sound to achieve a particular effect, for example: 'the dribbling dart of love' (1.3.2); 'every pelting, petty officer' (2.2.116).

Assonance: The repetition of a particular vowel sound in words close to each other to achieve a particular effect, for example: 'thick-ribbed ice', 'age, ache, penury' (3.1.123 and 130).

Enjambement: If blank verse was completely regular it would become boring. One way of varying the sound of blank verse is the use of enjambement, where the sense of the words runs on beyond the end of a line as in the example below:

CLAUDIO   ... Our natures do pursue
           Like rats that ravin down their proper bane
           A thirsty evil, and when we drink, we die
           (1.1.110–12)

Caesura: A deliberate break within or at the end of a line of verse, usually signalled by punctuation, for example:

ISABELLA   Tomorrow? Oh, that's sudden! Spare him, spare him!
           (2.2.85)

DEVELOPING YOUR IDEAS

2 Identify the speaker of each quotation below and give your view of how the language used reveals aspects of their character or their mood at that point in the play. For example, an image might show a particular attitude towards lechery or the movement of the verse might reveal a degree of emotional disturbance.

	QUOTATION	CHARACTER	WHAT IT SHOWS
A	For you must know, we have with special soul / Elected him our absence to supply, / Lent him our terror, dressed him with our love, / And given his deputation all the organs / Of our own power. What think you of it? (1.1.17–21)	Duke	The Duke is very conscious of his power (hence 'our' four times in four lines) even when relinquishing it. His reliance on abstract nouns like absence, terror, love, deputation and power make him seem removed from direct involvement.
B	There is a vice that most I do abhor, / And most desire should meet the blow of justice; / For which I would not plead, but that I must, / For which I must not plead, but that I am / At war 'twixt will and will not. (2.2.30–34)		
C	Who will believe thee, Isabel? / My unsoil'd name, th'austereness of my life, / My vouch against you, and my place i'th'state, / Will so your accusation overweigh / That you shall stifle in your own report / And smell of calumny. (2.4.155–60)		
D	Marry, this Claudio is condemned for untrussing. Farewell, good friar, I prithee, pray for me. The Duke, I say to thee again, would eat mutton on Fridays. He's not past it yet – and I say to thee – he would mouth with a beggar though she smelt brown bread and garlic – say that I said so – farewell. (3.2.152–7)		
E	Oh, your desert speaks loud, and I should wrong it, / To lock it in the wards of covert bosom / When it deserves with characters of brass / A forted residence 'gainst the tooth of time / And razure of oblivion. (5.1.9–13)		

 CONTINUED

Answers can be found at: www.hoddereducation.co.uk/workbookanswers

3   Read this passage then match a comment from the table below with each of the numbers in the passage:

CLAUDIO ... And the new deputy now for the Duke –
Whether it be the fault and glimpse of newness,
Or whether [1] that the body public be
A horse whereon the governor doth ride,[2]
Who, newly in the seat, that it may know
He can command, lets it straight feel the spur;[3]
Whether the tyranny be in his place,
Or in his eminence [4] that fills it up,
I stagger in [5] – but this new governor
Awakes me all the enrollèd penalties
Which have, like unscoured armour,[6] hung by th'wall
So long that nineteen zodiacs have gone round
And none of them been worn; and for a name
Now puts the drowsy and neglected Act [7]
Freshly on me: 'tis surely for a name.

LUCIO I warrant it is; and thy head stands so tickle on thy shoulders [8] that a milkmaid, if she be in love, may sigh it off. Send after the Duke and appeal to him. [9]
(1.2.138–55)

		NUMBER
A	Prose rather than verse, emphasising the contrast between the two speakers in terms of status and seriousness.	
B	The triple syllables have a grandness about them that contrasts with the short surrounding words.	
C	The enjambement carries forward Claudio's indignation, building emphasis on the object pronoun.	
D	The simile has overtones of battles fought long ago.	
E	An image of execution that is typical of the play's juxtaposition of comic and tragic.	
F	The rhythm of the verse 'staggers' to a stop mid-line along with the bewildered Claudio.	
G	The image of a rider exerting command over the untamed stallion of state by using his spurs creates a powerful impression of Angelo's rule. Claudio fears he might well be ridden down.	
H	Alliterative 's' monosyllables have a sharp sound that fits with the cruel jab of a spur.	
I	Repetition of 'whether' (three times in six lines) emphasises Claudio's uncertainty.	

4   What would be the effect on an audience of Shakespeare's use of language in the extract above?

....
....
....
....
....
....
....

KEY SKILLS

You will gain no credit for merely identifying a literary technique. You need to weave your identification of a technique into your analysis of its effect.

5   Match each quotation below to the literary technique of which it is an example and evaluate its effect on audiences. Choose from:

Metaphor   **Simile**   Personification   **Rhetorical question**   Alliteration

Enjambement   Repetition   **Chiasmus**   Caesura   Paradox

Remember that sometimes more than one technique is used.

QUOTATION	LITERARY TECHNIQUE AND ITS EFFECT
A ANGELO: When I would pray and think, I think and pray To several subjects (2.4.1–2)	
B DUKE: … If thou art rich th'art poor (3.1.28)	
C ISABELLA: Th'impression of keen whips I'd wear as rubies And strip myself to death as to a bed (2.4.101–2)	
D DUKE: … the very stream of his life and the business he hath helmed must upon a warranted need give him a better proclamation. (3.2.122–4)	
E ISABELLA: … ask your heart what it doth know That's like my brother's fault. (2.2.141–2)	
F ANGELO: What's this? What's this? Is this her fault or mine? (2.2.167)	
G DUKE: Thou art not noble; … Thou art not thyself; … Thou art not certain (3.1.13–23)	

CONTINUED ➡

Answers can be found at: www.hoddereducation.co.uk/workbookanswers

H ISABELLA: To whom should I complain? Did I tell this Who would believe me? (2.4.172–3)	
QUOTATION	**LITERARY TECHNIQUE AND ITS EFFECT**
I CLAUDIO: ...the delighted spirit To bathe in fiery floods or to reside In thrilling region of thick-ribbed ice (3.1.121–3)	
J ISABELLA: ... You granting of my suit, If that be sin, I'll make it my morn-prayer To have it added to the faults of mine (2.4.70–2)	

Metaphor: A figure of speech which compares one thing to another, without using the words 'as' or 'like', for example: 'the dribbling dart of love' (1.3.2). (Metaphor often has a symbolic dimension while similes are more direct.)

Simile: A figure of speech in which one thing is compared to another using the words 'like' or 'as', for example: 'Even like an o'er-grown lion in a cave / That goes not out to prey' (1.3.23–4).

Rhetorical questions: Questions for which the answer is not required, expected or important, for example: 'Condemn the fault, and not the actor of it?' (2.2.38).

Chiasmus: Parallel clauses in which the order of terms in the first one is reversed in the second, for example:

ISABELLA ... let your reason serve
To make the truth appear where it seems hid,
And hide the false seems true.

(5.1.65–7)

KEY SKILLS

Interpreting images

Analysing imagery is not an exact science. You will gain credit for your own interpretation of an image's effect on an audience, providing you make a persuasive case based on precise detail.

6 Find further examples for the table below and make your own comments on what each group of images contributes to the play.

IMAGE	EXAMPLES FROM THE PLAY	WHAT THE IMAGE REPRESENTS OR EXPRESSES
A Metal coinage, which can be weighed, tested, spent and possibly counterfeited	ANGELO: Let there be some more test made of my metal Before so noble and so great a figure Be stamped upon it. (1.1.48–9)	Money is not just a commercial convenience: it reflects honesty and trust. Coins stamped with the ruler's image are a symbol of that society and counterfeiting betrays a community's trust.

CONTINUED ➡

B	Horse training and riding	CLAUDIO: Or whether that the body public be A horse whereon the governor doth ride, Who, newly in the seat, that it may know He can command, lets it straight feel the spur; (1.2.140–43)	
C	Weighing on scales, especially those of justice	ISABELLA: We cannot weigh our brother with ourself. (2.2.130)	
D	Bawdiness, including prostitution, fornication and venereal disease	ISABELLA: I am come to know your pleasure. (2.4.31)	

7   Write a paragraph commenting on the humour of the passage below and then explain how Elbow contributes to the play's major themes.

> **ELBOW** If it please your honour, I am the poor Duke's constable, and my name is Elbow: I do lean upon justice, sir, and do bring in here, before your good honour, two notorious benefactors.
>
> (2.1.45–7)

....

....

....

....

....

....

Malapropisms: The term 'malapropism' was created for Sheridan's character Mrs Malaprop in the eighteenth century, but the phenomenon existed long before. It is the humorous misuse or distortion of a word or phrase, deliberately on the part of Shakespeare but unwittingly on the part of a character. Elbow is a master of the art of using words which don't have the meaning that he intends but which sound similar to words that do.

CONTINUED

Answers can be found at: www.hoddereducation.co.uk/workbookanswers

8   Read the extracts from two student comments below on sexual imagery in *Measure for Measure*. Annotate the responses to show the strengths A–D listed below. Then, on the following page, decide which you think would gain the higher mark and explain your choice.

A   Accurate uses of literary terminology

B   Fluently embedded quotations

C   Effective references to language without direct quotation

D   Effective analysis of language

Student 1:

> This is a play full of sexual images. When anyone says anything it probably has a sexual undertone, even if it is not obvious. Isabella's greeting to Angelo 'I come to know your pleasure' sounds innocent enough but would have had the groundlings nudging each other at the naughty possibilities. Some characters, such as Pompey, talk about sex through country images – 'groping for trout in a peculiar river' whilst Lucio uses food as his image, claiming that the Duke 'would eat mutton on Fridays' and 'mouth with a beggar though she smelt brown bread and garlic'.

Student 2:

> Shakespeare's use of a range of sexual images creates the dramatic background of lust and licence that pervades the play. There is no sex on stage of course; the sex is in the images and ideas rather than in the action. Once an audience has laughed at Lucio's puns on French velvet and syphilis, heard Pompey talk of 'groping for trout in a peculiar river' and seen pregnant Julietta, everything seems to have a sexual implication. Even Isabella's seemingly innocent greeting, 'I come to know your pleasure', is fraught with sexual tension.

CONTINUED ➡

....

....

....

....

....

....

....

....

....

....

TAKING IT FURTHER

9   Re-read the extract below and write a paragraph explaining how far you agree with the claim that the battle between these two characters is represented in the language.

ISABELLA	Must he needs die?
ANGELO	Maiden, no remedy.
ISABELLA	Yes: I do think that you might pardon him,
	And neither heaven nor man grieve at the mercy.
ANGELO	I will not do't.
ISABELLA	But can you, if you would?
ANGELO	Look, what I will not, that I cannot do.
ISABELLA	But might you do't, and do the world no wrong,
	If so your heart were touched with that remorse
	As mine is to him?
ANGELO	He's sentenced, 'tis too late.
LUCIO	[*To ISABELLA*] You are too cold.
ISABELLA	Too late? why, no; I, that do speak a word
	May call it again. Well, believe this:
	No ceremony that to great ones longs,
	Not the king's crown, nor the deputed sword,
	The marshal's truncheon, nor the judge's robe,
	Become them with one half so good a grace

CONTINUED ➡

     Answers can be found at: www.hoddereducation.co.uk/workbookanswers

As mercy does.

If he had been as you, and you as he,

You would have slipped like him, but he like you

Would not have been so stern.

ANGELO   Pray you be gone.
(2.2.48–68)

....

....

....

....

....

....

....

....

....

Challenge yourself

How far do you agree with the view expressed below by J. W. Lever (1965)? Compare his view with what other critics have said about the quality of poetry in the play.

The dramatic poetry of the first half of the play, with its free-ranging esemplastic imagery and flexible speech rhythms, gave way to sententious prose, stiff gnomic couplets and a blank verse which, though generally dignified, was basically uninspired.

Esemplastic: Having the imaginative power to bring disparate elements into a unified whole.

Gnomic: Writing that sounds wise but is not easily understood.

Contexts

In the exam, you will need to demonstrate an understanding of 'the significance and influence of the contexts in which literary texts are written and received' (AO3). You will also need to show through your argument and analysis how historical, social and cultural/literary contexts have **influenced and shaped** the ideas and methods in the play and the responses of audiences over time.

STARTING OUT

1   Look at the list of ten contextual factors in the box below. Categorise them in relation to their significance in influencing how Shakespeare wrote *Measure for Measure*. Use the rating below:

   A   Very significant

   B   Significant

   C   Not very significant

CONTEXTUAL FACTORS	SIGNIFICANCE	
I KING JAMES King James I was on the throne and had written a book on kingship. He did not like being surrounded by crowds. He was instrumental in ensuring that England signed a peace treaty with Spain in 1604.		
II THE ROLE OF WOMEN Daughters were expected to obey their fathers, and wives their husbands. Women were expected to be pure, prior to marriage; men were not. Women, apart from widows, could not own property.		
III THE JACOBEAN THEATRE Shakespeare's company had become 'The King's Men'. Female parts were played by young male actors. The design of The Globe meant that the audience were close to the stage and 'groundlings' paid one penny to stand, watch and cheer or jeer a performance.		
IV THE CITY OF VIENNA Vienna is recognisably seventeenth-century London, with the name changed to protect the playwright from censorship. Sexually transmitted diseases were often the focus of jokes on London stages and brothels were housed in the suburbs rather than the city.		
V CHRISTIANITY England was a Christian, officially Protestant, country. The Bible had been translated into English during the Reformation. Matthew's Gospel includes the idea of measure for measure in judgement.		
VI MARRIAGE An engagement to be married could be ended if a dowry was not forthcoming but in non-Catholic England a verbal contract was seen as sufficient for a marriage to be lawful.		

CONTINUED ➔

VII PURITANISM	
Puritans, who had been known as 'Precisionists', regarded theatres as dens of vice and were seeking to close them down as Shakespeare was writing *Measure for Measure*.	
VIII THE LAW	
In local areas, citizen constables were responsible for upholding the law, but these town constables were notoriously ineffective. Common people were hanged but gentlemen were lucky enough to be beheaded.	
IX CATHOLICISM	
Vienna was the Catholic capital city of the Holy Roman Empire. Virgin martyrs were honoured in the Catholic tradition but there were no longer any nunneries or friaries in England at the time that Shakespeare was writing.	
X SOURCES	
The story of Shakespeare's original source, Cinthio's tale, was well known, as was Shakespeare's main source, Whetstone's 1578 play, *Promos and Cassandra*. So too were the classical story of the disguised ruler Severus and Machiavelli's 1513 book, *The Prince*, a cynical guide to statecraft.	

DEVELOPING YOUR IDEAS

2 (a) Write a brief justification for your categorisation of each factor you rated as 'very significant'.

....

....

....

(b) Write a brief justification for your categorisation of any factor you rated as 'not very significant'.

....

....

....

3 Look up the quotations below and explain how each relates to social, cultural/literary or historical context. The first has been done for you.

	QUOTATION	RELATION TO CONTEXT
A	DUKE: ... I love the people / But do not like to stage me to their eyes (1.1.67–8)	James I was notoriously reluctant to be surrounded by crowds, however supportive they may have appeared.
B	MISTRESS OVERDONE: Thus, what with the war, what with the sweat, what with the gallows, and what with poverty, I am custom shrunk. (1.2.67)	

CONTINUED →

C	CLAUDIO: Thus stands it with me: upon a true contract / I got possession of Julietta's bed: / You know the lady; she is fast my wife, / Save that we do the denunciation lack / Of outward order (1.2.126–30)	
D	DUKE: ... Sith 'twas my fault to give the people scope, / 'Twould be my tyranny to strike and gall them / For what I bid them do (1.3.36–8)	
E	DUKE: ... Lord Angelo is precise; / Stands at a guard with envy; scarce confesses / That his blood flows, or that his appetite / Is more to bread than stone (1.3.51–4)	
F	ISABELLA: ... wishing a more strict restraint / Upon the sisterhood, the votarists of Saint Clare. (1.4.4–5)	
G	ESCALUS: Alas, it hath been great pains to you. They do you wrong to put you so oft upon't: are there not men in your ward sufficient to serve it? (2.1.226–8)	
H	ANGELO: ... Be that you are, / That is, a woman; if you be more, you're none; (2.4.135–6)	
I	DUKE: ... here, by this, is your brother saved, your honour untainted, the poor Mariana advantaged, and the corrupt deputy scaled. (3.1.237)	
J	DUKE: ... An Angelo for Claudio, death for death; / Haste still pays haste, and leisure answers leisure; / Like doth quit like, and measure still for measure. (5.1.401–4)	

4 (a) Take three of the quotations above, one historical, one social and one literary/cultural, remembering that such categories are not totally distinct. Suggest for each how it could have influenced perceptions of the play in Shakespeare's time, and how it might influence audiences now.

QUOTATION	THEN	NOW
Historical		
Social		
Cultural/Literary		

CONTINUED ➡

Answers can be found at: www.hoddereducation.co.uk/workbookanswers

(b) The following could be seen as evidence of the influence of historical context. Rate each one in terms of its dramatic significance. Circle 1 for low, 5 for high.

CONTEXTUAL INFLUENCE		RATING
A	Locating the drama outside England in a Catholic country and having Isabella as a novitiate of St Clare's	1 2 3 4 5
B	Focusing on the role of the ruler (James I?) in caring for his subjects: 'I love the people ...'	1 2 3 4 5
C	Making 'prenzie' Angelo a puritanical hypocrite whose blood is 'very snow-broth'	1 2 3 4 5

(c) The following could be seen as evidence of the influence of social context. Rate each one in terms of its dramatic significance. Circle 1 for low, 5 for high.

CONTEXTUAL INFLUENCE		RATING
A	Having the low-life characters mirror higher status characters	1 2 3 4 5
B	Presentation of the position of women in a society where the power structures are dominated by men	1 2 3 4 5
C	Having the London underworld appear in Vienna, where the Duke has seen 'corruption boil and bubble till it hath overrun the stew'	1 2 3 4 5

(d) The following could be seen as evidence of the influence of literary/cultural context. Rate each one in terms of its dramatic significance. Circle 1 for low, 5 for high.

CONTEXTUAL INFLUENCE		RATING
A	Greater focus on the role of the Duke than in the sources	1 2 3 4 5
B	The introduction of the 'bed trick' to preserve Isabella's virginity	1 2 3 4 5
C	The addition of Escalus as a foil for Angelo	1 2 3 4 5

KEY SKILLS

Incorporating context

To answer any question fully you need to take account of historical, social and cultural/literary context in relation to the author and to the audience. Build your awareness of context into your argument and resist the temptation to add references to context as an afterthought.

Challenge yourself

Read or watch the scenes in *Much Ado about Nothing* that include Dogberry (3.3 and 4.2). What similarities do you notice between Dogberry and Elbow?

5 (a) How successfully has social and historical context been incorporated into the following student paragraph about the presentation of women? Annotate the paragraph on the following page to show its strengths and weaknesses, then write an overall assessment.

CONTINUED ➡

'Measure for Measure' is a play that addresses the plight of women in Shakespeare's England in a way that a modern audience can admire. All the women in the play have real strengths – Isabella challenges Angelo's hypocrisy, Julietta defends her love for Claudio, Mariana is determined to regain Angelo and Mistress Overdone is a tough old bird who will endure. They need to be strong because in the seventeenth century the cards were all stacked against women – they could not own property, indeed they were the property of their fathers or husbands, and they were generally subject to male domination.

Your assessment:

....

....

....

....

....

....

....

....

....

....

(b) The following paragraph from a student essay about Angelo, misses several opportunities to weave in relevant social and historical context. Rewrite it, making the relevance of context clear.

Angelo is a villain and more devil than angel. He abuses the power he is given since once he sees and lusts after Isabella he realises that his blood is not 'snow-broth' after all. He then tries to avoid the consequences of his corrupt actions by bullying and by lying. When his attempt to brazen things out fails he asks for death rather than mercy and we wonder how Mariana can still be in love with such a hypocrite.

CONTINUED ➡

....
....
....
....
....
....
....
....

6   What merits can you find in the following extract from a student essay on humour in *Measure for Measure*? Annotate the response to show which of the strengths listed below you can identify.

A   Incorporation of contextual awareness

B   Fluently embedded quotations

C   Effective references to language without direct quotation

D   Effective analysis of language

E   Exploration of critical views

F   Perceptive analysis of key ideas

> Elbow is a genuinely amusing character, very similar in his 'misplacing' to
> Dogberry in 'Much Ado about Nothing' and likely to have been created for the
> company's established clown, Robert Armin. Jacobean audiences would have
> relished the way Shakespeare pokes fun at the incompetent town constable:
> Elbow has been in post for seven years because he does it for 'some piece
> of money' from his duty-avoiding fellow citizens. He is not merely amusing
> of course: his unsuccessful wrestling with words and meanings prompts
> Escalus (generally the most reliable moral guide we have) to pinpoint one of
> the key ideas in the play by asking, 'Which is wiser here, Justice or Iniquity?'

TAKING IT FURTHER

7 (a) It has been argued that *Measure for Measure* is a play of ideas rather than actions. Decide how much you agree or disagree with each claim below relating to a cultural concept, idea or belief. Circle 1 for strongly disagree, 5 for agree strongly.

CLAIM		RATING				
A	Women's chastity is shown by the bed-trick to be merely a commodity.	1	2	3	4	5
B	Puritanism is mocked by Pompey and exposed as inhuman by Angelo.	1	2	3	4	5
C	The Duke is presented as a God-like figure not a mere human being.	1	2	3	4	5
D	Human nature is shown to be more powerful than the law.	1	2	3	4	5
E	Marriage is made a mockery of when the Duke marries Isabella and marries off Lucio to Kate Keepdown.	1	2	3	4	5
F	Death is ever-present in the minds and mouths of the characters and therefore in the thoughts of the audience.	1	2	3	4	5
G	Apart from the title, Christianity contributes little to *Measure for Measure*.	1	2	3	4	5

(b) Choose the claim which you **disagreed** with most and write a paragraph explaining your disagreement. Cite the textual evidence that supports your view.

....

....

....

....

....

(c) Choose the claim which you **agreed** with most and write a paragraph explaining why you agreed with it. Cite the textual evidence that supports your view.

....

....

....

....

....

Challenge yourself

Research the life and reign of James I. Identify points that you think the original audience would have noted as featuring in *Measure for Measure*.

Answers can be found at: www.hoddereducation.co.uk/workbookanswers

8   We live in a world where women are no longer prepared to keep quiet about sexual harassment or the male abuse of power for sexual advantage. How do you think a modern audience might react differently from the original audience to the aspects of the play outlined below?

ASPECT	DIFFERENCES IN LIKELY AUDIENCE REACTIONS
Julietta being made pregnant by Claudio	
Angelo's attempt at sexual blackmail	
Isabella's refusal to save Claudio by losing her virginity	
Mariana's readiness to have sex with Angelo	
Isabella's reaction to the Duke's claiming of her hand in marriage	

9   Look at the following exam-style questions. For each question think about how you could include **two** purposeful points on the **significance and influence of contexts**. Write those two points in the space provided beneath each question.

   (a) **How far do you agree with the claim that Shakespeare's presentation of male authority was for his age and not for all time?**

   ●   Point 1: ....

   ....

   ....

   ●   Point 2: ....

   ....

   ....

   (b) **How far do you agree that the underworld of Vienna is presented as a distorted mirror image of the world of the higher status characters?**

   ●   Point 1: ....

   ....

   ....

   ●   Point 2. ....

   ....

   ....

Critical approaches

The good news is that there is no single correct interpretation of any Shakespeare play, or even of any character. Your challenge is to take into account the views of a range of critics (AO5) when developing your own interpretation of *Measure for Measure*.

STARTING OUT

1   What do you think about some of the key critical issues relating to *Measure for Measure*?

(a) Decide how to respond to the questions below. Circle the response closest to your initial reaction.

QUESTION		RESPONSE
A	Is the Duke a flawed human being struggling to develop self-knowledge rather than God's representative on earth, dispensing divine justice?	YES / PROBABLY / POSSIBLY / NO
B	Is Isabella a voice for the female right to choose her own destiny, not just a victim of male attitudes and power structures?	YES / PROBABLY / POSSIBLY / NO
C	Does *Measure for Measure* reflect Shakespeare's personal ideas and feelings rather than being a reflection of the ideology of his time?	YES / PROBABLY / POSSIBLY / NO
D	Are the low-life characters largely comic relief, rather than the representatives of an oppressed underclass who offer a carnivalesque challenge to the established social order?	YES / PROBABLY / POSSIBLY / NO
E	Is *Measure for Measure* 'masterly in stage-craft', not just a 'broken-backed' play of two halves?	YES / PROBABLY / POSSIBLY / NO
F	Is *Measure for Measure* as much a demonstration of the need for control as a condemnation of the corruption of power?	YES / PROBABLY / POSSIBLY / NO
G	Does *Measure for Measure* reinforce rather than challenge the idea of male domination?	YES / PROBABLY / POSSIBLY / NO
H	Is the play about achieving balance between opposites rather than any particular opposition such as justice vs mercy?	YES / PROBABLY / POSSIBLY / NO
I	Does the biblical reference in the title signal that *Measure for Measure* is essentially a Christian play?	YES / PROBABLY / POSSIBLY / NO
J	Does *Measure for Measure* have a potentially tragic first half and an unsatisfactorily comic second half?	YES / PROBABLY / POSSIBLY / NO

(b) Identify one of the questions you agreed with and explain why.

....

....

....

(c) Identify one of the questions you disagreed with and explain why.

....

....

....

CONTINUED

(d) What other questions do you think are worth asking?

....

....

....

DEVELOPING YOUR IDEAS

2   Below are various critics' views on *Measure for Measure*. The fact that they differ so markedly should help to remind you that no critic is likely to be right (or wrong) all the time.

(a) Write a paragraph in which you challenge Coleridge's view of *Measure for Measure*.

Measure for Measure ... is a hateful work, although Shakespearean throughout. Our feelings of justice are grossly wounded in Angelo's escape. Isabella herself contrives to be unamiable, and Claudio is detestable.

(Samuel Taylor Coleridge)

....

....

....

....

....

....

(b) How far do you agree with the view expressed below?

The play ... rightly condemns Angelo's behavior, alongside the hypocritical society that lets him get away with it, even as it contends with the fact that, ultimately, Isabella's harassment is part of a much wider issue: human beings constantly falling short of the standards they set for themselves, and those in power being able to fall short with impunity. The true sexual immorality of Vienna turns out to be rooted not in sensuality, but in hypocrisy.

(Burton 2017)

....

....

....

....

....

....

CONTINUED ➡

(c) Consider and comment on G. Wilson Knight's claim below.

The play must be read in the light of the Gospel teaching if its full significance is to be apparent.

(Wilson Knight 1930)

....

....

....

....

....

....

(d) Using the quotations you have read in earlier parts of this question, write a paragraph in which you explore the significance of substitution in *Measure for Measure*.

....

....

....

....

....

....

(e) Does the view expressed below reinforce or modify your personal interpretation of the play? Explain why, referring to relevant textual evidence.

The Duke executes his power for no reason other than to reaffirm his authority. In fact, his power rests on his orchestration of artificial demonstrations such as this. 'Control of the threat becomes the rationale of authoritarian reaction in a time of apparent crisis' (Dollimore 73).

(Goldberg 2011)

....

....

....

....

....

....

....

KEY SKILLS

While it is possible to distinguish broad schools of thought in Shakespeare criticism, be wary of making sweeping statements such as, 'Feminist criticism would see Isabella as a passive victim of patriarchal forces'. It is more useful to begin with your own ideas on aspects of the play and to develop them in relation to different schools of critical thought.

3   In the table below, match each critical viewpoint in column 1 with a set of typical characteristics from column 2 and a quotation from column 3 in which critics of each school of critical thought might be especially interested.

CRITICAL VIEWPOINT	CHARACTERISTICS	QUOTATIONS
Historicist criticism	Viewing a text as a reflection of the socio-political conditions in which it was produced, especially in terms of class and power as seen by Marx.	ANGELO: … your grace, like power divine, Hath looked upon my passes. (5.1.362–3)
Feminist criticism	Seeing the text as a product of its historical, social and cultural context.	ANGELO: … What dost thou or what art thou, Angelo? Dost thou desire her foully for those things That make her good? (2.2.177–9)
Christian criticism	Seeing the text as expressing repressed desires and the conflict between them and social expectations.	DUKE: … I love the people But do not like to stage me to their eyes: (1.1.67–8)
Psychoanalytical criticism	Maintaining that gender is the basis of the play's argument and focusing particularly on the representation of women.	CLAUDIO: … Whether the tyranny be in his place, Or in his eminence that fills it up, I stagger in— (1.2.144–6)
Reader response criticism	Seeing the text as an exploration of divine justice and mercy as expressed in the Gospels.	Isabella's final silence (5.1)
Marxist criticism	Focusing on the reader's (or audience's) role in 'completing' a literary work through interpretation rather than focusing primarily on the author or the content and form of the work.	ANGELO: …. Be that you are That is, a woman; if you be more you're none. (2.4.135–6)

CONTINUED

Schools of critical thought

Feminist criticism

Feminist critics are interested in the representation of women in literature. They highlight, criticise and resist the patriarchal assumptions and gendered stereotypes in a text. Some feminist critics have read *Measure for Measure* as a play which conforms to male ideas and prejudices, while others think the play questions and subverts patriarchy.

4 (a) Think carefully about each statement in the table below and consider how far you agree (10 = agree the most).

STATEMENT ON THE PLAY FROM A FEMINIST PERSPECTIVE	DO YOU AGREE?
A Isabella's fate – condemned to a marriage she did not seek and about which she will not speak – is clear evidence of the marginalisation of women in a man's world.	/10
B Mariana conforms to the expectations of the time in her slavish affection for Angelo.	/10
C Mistress Overdone and Kate Keepdown are the exploited victims of male desire.	/10
D Patriarchal economic and social structures prohibit Isabella from challenging Angelo.	/10
E Men are portrayed as powerful; women are shown as powerless.	/10
F It is the female, not the male, characters who have the moral authority.	/10
G In the society of Vienna everything depends on decisions made by the males who control the power structures.	/10
H The bawdy jokes throughout the play expose the double standards in relation to women and sexuality.	/10

(b) Identify the statement you agreed with the most and explain why.

....

....

....

(c) Identify the statement you disagreed with the most and explain why.

....

....

....

(d) How far do you agree with view that *Measure for Measure* 'may be one of the most relevant plays ever written about sexual harassment and abuse against women, and the stakes for women who speak up about it' (Burton 2017)?

....

....

....

CONTINUED

Answers can be found at: www.hoddereducation.co.uk/workbookanswers

Marxist criticism

A Marxist approach to criticism claims that literary texts cannot be separated from their social and historical contexts. Marxist critics look at ways in which texts support or question prevailing contextual ideas or ideologies, specifically those related to political power and economics.

5 (a) Look at the extract below and underline points that you think would be of particular interest from the perspective of a Marxist critic:

> **DUKE** ... My business in this state
> Made me a looker-on here in Vienna,
> Where I have seen corruption boil and bubble
> Till it o'errun the stew; laws for all faults,
> But faults so countenanced that the strong statutes
> Stand like the forfeits in a barber's shop,
> As much in mock as mark.
>
> **ESCALUS** Slander to t'state!
> Away with him to prison!
> (5.1.312–19)

(b) What evidence would you cite to confirm **and/or** challenge the broadly Marxist view below?

The Duke is a **Machiavellian** authority figure, out to eliminate certain types of undesirable behaviour, not just on the part of the lower classes, and through covert surveillance to extend his grip on dictatorial power.

● Evidence for: ....

....

....

● Evidence against: ....

....

....

(c) If a production of *Measure for Measure* was (like the RSC production of 1998–9) set in a modern totalitarian state,
   (i) which aspects of the play would you expect the director to emphasise?

....

....

   (ii) which aspects of the play do you think would be most difficult to present on stage?

....

....

Ideology: originally an eighteenth-century term, it now means a system of ideas and ideals, or a set of economic or political beliefs, characteristic of a social group. For some Marxist writers it can mean the general process of the production of meanings and ideas.

Machiavellian: a cunning and unscrupulous approach to governing which puts power before principles and political expediency before morality. It refers to the book on statecraft by the sixteenth-century Italian writer Niccolo Machiavelli, which some say is still relevant today.

CONTINUED ➡

Christian criticism

G. Wilson Knight in the 1930s drew attention to the Christian dimension of *Measure for Measure*. Not only did he focus on the title's biblical origin – 'Judge not that ye be not judged' (Matthew 7.1) – he saw the Duke as a God-like figure and Isabella as symbolising the Christian virtue of mercy.

6 (a)   How do think an audience in 1604 would have seen the Christian elements of the play?

....

....

....

....

   (b)   How might a modern audience see those elements?

....

....

Historicist criticism

Some exam boards, particularly AQA, make it clear that they expect you to be aware of historicist approaches to texts: the view that no text exists in isolation but is the product of the time in which it was produced. This approach encourages you to explore the relationships that exist between texts and the contexts within which they are written, received and understood.

For example, if exploring Angelo and Isabella's relationship, you are expected to engage not only with contexts of gender, power, morality and society, but also with the contexts of when texts were written and how they have been received.

7   Which of the aspects of interpretation below do you think you would **not** be relevant when writing about Angelo and Isabella from the historicist perspective?

   A   Expectations of male and female behaviour from a seventeenth-century perspective; for example, Angelo's perversion of the traditional courtship rituals

   B   How attitudes to men and women and their respective roles might have changed over time

   C   The way that the Harvey Weinstein case enables us to see that the moral issues of Shakespeare's time are similar to those of our own

   D   The fact that Isabella's arguments might be seen as being inspired by Christian ideals whereas Angelo might be interpreted as a Puritan

   E   The Renaissance notion of the bodily humours and therefore that Angelo's excess of blood could be affecting his behaviour and/or modern ideas about psychology and sexual repression

   F   The view that traditions in literary study are themselves context-bound and locked into changing critical and cultural approaches

Psychoanalytical criticism

8   Using the internet, research the Freudian concepts of ego and id. Then write a paragraph explaining how far you agree with the claim below:

> Angelo has a highly developed super-ego, meaning that he believes he is impervious to temptation. However his id, representing his inner desires, is powerfully awakened by Isabella, and, unwilling to lose his reputation, he bullies Isabella into giving in to him, rather than proposing to her openly.
>
> (Crowe 2017)

....

....

CONTINUED ➡

....

....

....

....

Reader response criticism

9 Isabella's silence at the end of Act 5 has been, and can be, interpreted in different ways by different audiences. Comment on how it might have been interpreted by the audiences listed below:

(a) Watchers of the court performance of *Measure for Measure* in 1604

....

....

(b) People who saw Peter Brook's 1950 production

....

....

(c) An audience at The Globe in 2018

....

....

....

10 In his book *Literary Theory* (1983), Terry Eagleton wrote that all literary texts has been 'rewritten' by those who read them 'if only unconsciously'.

(a) On a separate piece of paper, write your personal response to the claim made by Eagleton with reference to *Measure for Measure*.

(b) Decide which of the critical perspectives outlined in this section have had the greatest influence on your own interpretation of *Measure for Measure*. On a separate piece of paper, write a critical analysis of the passage below relating your ideas to this critical reading.

DUKE VINCENTIO	[To ISABELLA] If he be like your brother, for his sake Is he pardoned; and, for your lovely sake, Give me your hand, and say you will be mine, He is my brother too. But fitter time for that. By this Lord Angelo perceives he's safe; Methinks I see a quick'ning in his eye. Well, Angelo, your evil quits you well. Look that you love your wife: her worth, worth yours. I find an apt remission in myself; And yet here's one in place I cannot pardon. [To LUCIO] You, sirrah, that knew me for a fool, a coward, One all of luxury, an ass, a madman: Wherein have I so deserved of you That you extol me thus?
LUCIO	'Faith, my lord. I spoke it but according to the trick. If you will hang me for it, you may – but I had rather it would please you I might be whipped.

CONTINUED ➡

DUKE VINCENTIO	Whipped first, sir, and hanged after.
	Proclaim it, provost, round about the city:
	If any woman wronged by this lewd fellow,
	As I have heard him swear himself there's one
	Whom he begot with child, let her appear,
	And he shall marry her. The nuptial finish'd,
	Let him be whipped and hanged.
LUCIO	I beseech your highness, do not marry me to a whore.
	Your highness said, even now, I made you a duke: good
	my lord, do not recompense me in making me a cuckold.
DUKE VINCENTIO	Upon mine honour, thou shalt marry her.
	Thy slanders I forgive, and therewithal
	Remit thy other forfeits: Take him to prison;
	And see our pleasure herein executed.
LUCIO	Marrying a punk, my lord, is pressing to death, whipping,
	and hanging!
DUKE VINCENTIO	Slandering a prince deserves it.
	(5.1.483 –516)

Challenge yourself

Read the essay on *Measure for Measure* by F. R. Leavis in *The Common Pursuit* written in 1952. Identify what you think are its strengths and weaknesses as a critical response to the play.

Boosting your skills

This first section focuses on how you can approach the different types of question you might encounter in the exam. Later sections help you to develop and refine your essay writing skills.

STARTING OUT

Assessment Objectives

1   Draw a line to match the skills with the AS/A-level English Literature Assessment Objectives. There may be more than one skill for each Assessment Objective.

Skills		Assessment Objectives
The accuracy and fluency of your writing		AO1
Demonstrating an awareness that there is more than one way to interpret the play		
Making links between the play and another literary text		AO2
Creating and developing an argument and a clear structure		
Showing an understanding of the importance and influence of contexts		AO3
Using literary terms and concepts		
		AO4
Allowing other readings – including those from critics or statements given in the exam – to influence your own interpretation		
Analysing meanings and how they are shaped by language		AO5
Showing an understanding that the play can be understood differently by audiences and readers over time		

KEY SKILLS

There are important differences between exam boards and specifications and also, in some cases, between the AS and the A-level exams. Ensure you know which of the Assessment Objectives apply to the *Measure for Measure* question you will be answering in the exam or for your Non-Examined Assessment (coursework).

Understanding the Assessment Objectives

2   The Assessment Objectives (AOs) are written in examiner-speak. Look up the way they are defined and described in the specification you are studying, then write a note to yourself in student-speak on each AO to help you remember what each one means and what it includes, with examples.

- AO1: Articulate informed, personal and creative responses to literary texts, using associated concepts and terminology, and coherent, accurate written expression.

....

....

- AO2: Analyse ways in which meanings are shaped in literary texts.

....

....

- AO3: Demonstrate understanding of the significance and influence of the contexts in which literary texts are written and received.

....

....

- AO4: Explore connections across literary texts.

....

....

- AO5: Explore literary texts informed by different interpretations.

....

....

Significance: 'Significance' involves weighing up all the potential contributions to a textual analysis; for example, through the way the text is constructed and written, through text-specific contexts that can be relevantly applied, through connecting the text(s) to other texts and then finding potential meanings and interpretations.

KEY SKILLS

Command words

Command words in questions tell you how to respond to a particular task, and they appear as part of a phrase, for example: 'discuss how Shakespeare presents X'.

Here is a list of command words used across examination boards. You need to know exactly what each of these means; for example, you need to understand the difference between 'analyse' and 'explore'.

- Analyse: separate information into components and identify their characteristics.
- Compare and contrast: identify similarities and differences.
- Discuss: present key points about different ideas or strengths and weaknesses of an idea.
- Examine: investigate closely.
- Explore: investigate without preconceptions about the outcome.

Reading the questions

The first challenge you meet in the examination is finding the relevant question and reading what is required of you. That becomes easier if you understand the code in which examination questions are written. The key to that code is the use of command words by examiners to signal what they expect as a response. Examiners are not out to trick you, and the command words used by a particular exam board are consistent across time.

3   Although all the specifications address the same Assessment Objectives, question styles vary across exam boards. You need to check on the question style of your exam board by looking at past papers and specimen papers. The example questions below are from different boards.

(a) Interpreting a question which includes an extract:

'Typically, texts about relationships are presented from a male point of view.'
In the light of this view, discuss how Shakespeare presents the relationship between Angelo and Isabella in this extract and elsewhere in the play. (AQA style)

Unpacking the requirements of a question such as the one above reveals how systematically the AOs are addressed. In the table below draw a line to the explanation which matches each command word:

'Typically **(1)**, texts about relationships are presented from a male point of view.'
In the light of this view, discuss **(2)** how **(3)** Shakespeare presents the relationship
(4) between Angelo and Isabella in this extract and elsewhere in the play.

COMMAND WORD		EXPLANATION
1 Typically		A As you discuss, you need not only to organise your writing and use appropriate terminology (AO1) but also to take account of different interpretations, rather than follow a single-track argument (AO5).
2 Discuss		B In exploring Angelo's relationship with Isabella, you need to engage with contexts of gender, power and society along with contexts of production and reception (AO3).
3 How		B In engaging in the debate about the 'typicality' of the view, you will be addressing AO5. As you are discussing the typicality of the view, you need to connect with one of the central issues of 'Love through the ages' and so with the representation of relationships in other texts (AO4).
4 Relationship		
		D The words 'how Shakespeare presents' signal an invitation to you to write about Shakespeare's dramatic methods (AO2).

Note that the above question requires you to address the extract **and** relevant sections from the rest of the play, but **not** to try to write about the whole play.

(b) Interpreting a general question about the whole play:

Explore Shakespeare's presentation of X in *Measure for Measure*. You must relate your discussion to relevant contextual factors and ideas from your critical reading. (Edexcel style)

Explore **(1)** Shakespeare's presentation **(2)** of X in *Measure for Measure*.**(3)** You must relate your discussion **(4)** to relevant contextual factors **(5)** and ideas from your critical reading.**(6)**

'X' here could be a theme / idea, character / relationship, significant technique or distinctive approach. In the table on the following page identify which explanation matches each of the numbered words or phrases in the question above:

CONTINUED ➤

1	Explore		A	This explicitly requires reference to a range of critical ideas and perspectives.
2	Presentation		B	This term tells you that you need to organise your writing and use appropriate terminology (AO1) and to take account of different interpretations rather than follow a single-track argument (AO5).
3	*Measure for Measure*		C	This means consider and analyse a range of ideas and issues relating to the play (AO1).
4	Discussion		D	This means you need to engage with contexts of gender, power and society along with contexts of production and reception (AO3).
5	Relevant contextual factors		E	The title signals that the expected response would need to range across the whole play.
6	Ideas from your critical reading		F	This signals an invitation to you to write about Shakespeare's dramatic methods (AO2).

Presentation: A question reference to 'presentation' reminds you to consider aspects of structure and language use.

4   Creating questions of your own is a good way to get into the examiner's mindset. Look at past questions for the exam board you will be sitting and use those as your model.

(a) Write your own essay question on a **theme** in the play, using appropriate command words.

....

....

....

....

(b) Write your own essay question on a **dramatic technique** in the play, using appropriate command words.

....

....

....

....

(c) Write your own essay question on a **significant relationship between two characters** in the play, using appropriate command words.

....

....

....

....

CONTINUED

Answers can be found at: www.hoddereducation.co.uk/workbookanswers

5   Look at the following exam questions and identify the exam board question that is relevant for you. Highlight and annotate it as you might in the exam. Use the approaches and questions in Question 3 to help you.

(a) Discuss how Shakespeare presents the Duke in his dual role as friar and as ruler. You must relate your discussion to relevant contextual factors and ideas from your critical reading. (Edexcel style)

(b) 'Ironically, the higher status characters generally have less appeal to an audience than the low-life characters.'
   In the light of this view, discuss how Shakespeare presents the relationship between the official world and the underworld of Vienna in this conversation between Escalus and Pompey (2.1.181–219) and elsewhere in the play. (AQA style)

(c) Discuss Act 5 Scene 1 lines 343–72 exploring Shakespeare's use of language and its dramatic effects.

(d) 'A play in which the abuse of power is held to account.'
   Using your knowledge of the play as a whole, show how far you agree with this view of *Measure for Measure*.
   Remember to support your answer with reference to different interpretations. (OCR style)

(e) With close reference to the language and imagery in this passage [Act 1 Scene 5 lines 160–91], examine how Shakespeare presents Angelo's state of mind.
   Consider the view that Shakespeare's presentation of the abuse of personal and political power in *Measure for Measure* has universal interest and relevance. (Eduqas style)

DEVELOPING YOUR IDEAS

Essay planning and structure (AO1)

6   The statements below are about what to do when **planning** an essay in the exam. Cross through the statements that are **not** likely to help you to write a successful essay on *Measure for Measure*.

NOTE: *Make sure you check your answers before proceeding to the subsequent activities.*

A   Don't spend too long planning – it is more important that you use the time writing a substantial essay.

B   Read the question carefully a number of times and underline key words and phrases, especially the command words.

C   Consider the order in which you can make your points and think how one point can lead on clearly to another.

D   If you have a choice of questions, read both questions carefully – don't just go with your initial instinct.

E   Spend some planning time trying to remember how you wrote a recent essay on a similar theme.

F   Do not worry about having a central argument – just start writing and hopefully you will have thought of one by the time you write your conclusion.

G   For each point, think about the evidence / quotations you can use to support it.

7   Even if you already have a preferred approach to planning essays, try the two approaches below to see which suits you.

   Examine the view that in *Measure for Measure* Isabella is 'a female character whose plight reflects that of all women'. You must relate your discussion to relevant contextual factors and ideas from your critical reading.

   (a)   Create a spider diagram with different points you could make in response to this question.

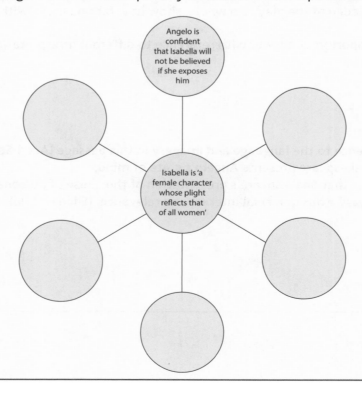

Angelo is confident that Isabella will not be believed if she exposes him

Isabella is 'a female character whose plight reflects that of all women'

CONTINUED ➡

(b) List points you could make in response to this question in the space below

- ....
- ....
- ....
- ....
- ....
- ....
- ....

(c) Which of the two approaches to planning did you prefer and why?

....
....

8   Look again at your spider diagram or list for Question 7. Read this Edexcel-style question:

Explore how Shakespeare presents relationships between the sexes in *Measure for Measure*. **You must relate your discussion to relevant contextual factors and ideas from your critical reading.**

Make notes on how you could answer this question. Identify:

- particular dramatic moments

....
....

- key quotations

....
....

- relevant contextual factors

....
....

- appropriate critical ideas.

....
....

KEY SKILLS

There is no set number of points you need or are advised to make in an exam essay for AS/A-level English Literature, but if you have more than six relevant, developed points you risk losing focus. If you have made more than six points in your spider diagram, see if any points are weak, lack potential or could perhaps be combined.

Introductions

Introductory paragraphs are important: examiners very quickly begin to build an impression of the kind of candidate you are. Although they are always ready to revise that first impression, why not convince them of your ability early on?

CONTINUED

9   Below are two introductory paragraphs to the exam-style question in Question 8. Decide which is the more effective.

(A) Shakespeare presents the relationships between the sexes very effectively in the play. We see a wide range of relationships, from virginal horror at the prospect of defilement to lewd delight in lechery. Most of the play is about sex – not physical on stage of course, but in the mind, heart and loins of the characters. The low-life characters are very open about sexual relationships as being a commercial transaction and ironically sex becomes a price demanded by the higher status characters too. The only genuinely loving relationship seems to be that of Claudio and Julietta – the others finish up married for life but not for love.

(B) 'You will needs buy and sell men and women like beasts' is an accusation against Pompey, put in the malapropic mouth of Elbow, but it serves as a summary of the way relationships between the sexes are presented in 'Measure for Measure'. Bodies are bargaining chips; the imagery of coins and coining is threaded through the play – whether it be Kate Keepdown's abused body or the previously virginal Mariana. Shakespeare does offer us reference points, with Julietta embodying love at one extreme, insisting on her sin having been committed 'mutually', and Lucio at the other extreme cheerfully acknowledging his unloving lust. Ironically the reward (or punishment) for both loving and lusting is the same – marriage.

Outline the reasons for your preference and suggest two ways in which the less effective one could be improved.

....

....

....

....

....

....

....

....

KEY SKILLS

Presenting an argument

AO1 states that you will be assessed on your ability to demonstrate a 'personal' response to *Measure for Measure*. Examiners note that a marked feature of top-level responses is presenting a clear and consistent argument, established in the opening paragraph, sustained and developed in the main body of the essay and revisited in the conclusion.

Linking your points

There are a number of ways in which you can link paragraphs. Using markers such as 'on the other hand' and 'in a similar way' can be a very effective way to begin paragraphs.

If you carry on an idea into a second paragraph, you could begin with '**Moreover**, Angelo's hypocrisy can also be seen in …'. You could challenge the preceding paragraph by starting with '**On the other hand**, this view of Angelo can be challenged from a feminist perspective…'.

Challenge yourself

A high-grade response might, if appropriate, be able **integrate** an important **context** or **critical perspective** in the argument/opening paragraph. Write an introduction to the question below with this in mind.

'The play is an unsatisfactory mixture of tragic and comic.'

How far and in what ways do you agree with this view of *Measure for Measure*?

Concluding (AO1)

Conclusions matter: they are your final opportunity to influence the examiner as s/he decides what mark to award you, so avoid starting your conclusion with a vague, self-congratulatory phrase such as, 'As I believe I have shown convincingly throughout this essay'.

10 (a) Read the three statements below about writing conclusions. Tick any you believe to be good advice.

    A The conclusion needs to be long enough to summarise your answer.

    B The conclusion should correlate in some way with your argument.

    C The conclusion should end with a flourish – a compelling end to your essay.

(b) Listed below are a number of different ways to conclude an essay on *Measure for Measure*. How you conclude will depend on the Assessment Objectives being examined for your course. Some of these methods may well be combined.

Give each suggestion a score out of 10 (10 = agree the most).

SUGGESTED TECHNIQUE		DO YOU AGREE?
A	Ending with a compelling quotation that makes the reader think, such as 'Which is wiser here, justice or inquity?' or perhaps a quotation from a critic you have learnt.	/10
B	Ending with a twist: present a stark, interesting alternative view from the one you have been expressing in the rest of the essay.	/10
C	Confirming why you think the character, theme, issue or technique under discussion is fundamental to the play.	/10
D	Reminding the examiner that your career could depend on her/his decision about your mark, and that you have done your best.	/10
E	Providing a balanced overview of the main points you have made.	/10
F	Mentioning how audiences in 1604 might have responded differently from a twenty-first-century audience.	/10
G	Returning to points and phrases you made in your introduction to give the essay a satisfying cohesion.	/10

Select one of the above methods (or perhaps a combination) which you rated highly and write your conclusion to one or two of the questions you have been planning in this section.

....

....

....

....

....

....

....

CONTINUED ➡

....

....

....

11 (a) Look through the sequence of points below which outline an approach to planning essays. Highlight or underline the ones that you think would be helpful:

A If you have a choice of questions, read them both carefully before deciding which to answer.

B Highlight and annotate the question to ensure you are really clear what you are being asked to do.

C Create a spider diagram or write a list of potential points you could make to answer the question.

D Select the points you want to make; be prepared to discard repeated or less successful points.

E Think about and jot down evidence / quotations, context and, where relevant, critical viewpoints and perspectives.

F Decide on the order of points.

G Refine and confirm what your core argument is going to be; this may well end up being part of your introduction.

H Check to ensure all points clearly answer the question.

(b) Follow the sequence above as you plan responses to one or more of the following exam questions. Complete points A–H above in no more than **15 minutes** for each question. Start below, and continue on a separate piece of paper.

Explore Shakespeare's presentation of time in *Measure for Measure*. You must relate your discussion to relevant contextual factors and ideas from your critical reading.

Explore Shakespeare's presentation of male characters in *Measure for Measure*. You must relate your discussion to relevant contextual factors and ideas from your critical reading.

....

....

....

....

....

....

....

(c) Some exam boards set questions, such as the ones below, which invite you to respond to a viewpoint or statement (AO5). These questions contain an interpretation of a particular aspect of the play, such as character, theme or structure. For some boards you need to provide your own take on the given statement in relation to an extract and to wider aspects of the play.

If you will be sitting a board which uses this type of question, use your preferred planning approach to plan answers to the questions on the following pages.

CONTINUED ➔

'The ending of *Measure for Measure* is conventional and convenient but never convincing.'
In the light of this view, discuss Shakespeare's presentation of the Duke in this extract from the
final scene and elsewhere in the play.

DUKE VINCENTIO	Come hither, Isabel.
	Your friar is now your prince: as I was then
	Advertising and holy to your business,
	Not changing heart with habit, I am still
	Attorneyed at your service.
ISABELLA	Oh, give me pardon
	That I, your vassal, have employed and pained
	Your unknown sovereignty.
DUKE VINCENTIO	You are pardoned, Isabel:
	And now dear maid, be you as free to us.
	Your brother's death I know sits at your heart,
	And you may marvel why I obscured myself,
	Labouring to save his life, and would not rather
	Make rash remonstrance of my hidden power
	Than let him so be lost. Oh, most kind maid,
	It was the swift celerity of his death
	Which I did think with slower foot came on
	That brained my purpose – but peace be with him.
	That life is better life, past fearing death,
	Than that which lives to fear: make it your comfort,
	So happy is your brother.
ISABELLA	I do, my lord.

[*Enter ANGELO, MARIANA, FRIAR PETER, and PROVOST*]

DUKE VINCENTIO	For this new-married man approaching here,
	Whose salt imagination yet hath wronged
	Your welledefended honour, you must pardon
	For Mariana's sake. But as he adjudged your brother,
	Being criminal in double violation
	Of sacred chastity and of promise-breach
	Thereon dependent for your brother's life,
	The very mercy of the law cries out
	Most audible, even from his proper tongue:
	An Angelo for Claudio, death for death;
	Haste still pays haste, and leisure answers leisure;
	Like doth quit like, and measure still for measure.
	Then, Angelo, thy fault's thus manifested
	Which, though thou wouldst deny, denies thee vantage.
	We do condemn thee to the very block
	Where Claudio stooped to death, and with like haste.
	Away with him.

(5.1.374-408)

CONTINUED →

**'Typically, texts present the male domination of women as inevitable rather than intolerable.'
In the light of this view, discuss how Shakespeare presents the relationship between Angelo and
Isabella in this extract and elsewhere in the play.**

ISABELLA	Oh, pardon me, my lord, it oft falls out To have what we would have, we speak not what we mean. I something do excuse the thing I hate For his advantage that I dearly love.
ANGELO	We are all frail.
ISABELLA	Else let my brother die, If not a fedary but only he Owe and succeed thy weakness.
ANGELO	Nay, women are frail too.
ISABELLA	Ay, as the glasses where they view themselves, Which are as easy broke as they make forms. Women? Help heaven, men their creation mar In profiting by them. Nay, call us ten times frail, For we are soft as our complexions are. And credulous to false prints.
ANGELO	I think it well, And from this testimony of your own sex – Since I suppose we are made to be no stronger Than faults may shake our frames – let me be bold; I do arrest your words. Be that you are, That is, a woman; if you be more, you're none. If you be one, as you are well expressed By all external warrants, show it now By putting on the destined livery.
ISABELLA	I have no tongue but one. Gentle my lord, Let me entreat you speak the former language.
ANGELO	Plainly conceive, I love you.
ISABELLA	My brother did love Juliet, And you tell me that he shall die for't.
ANGELO	He shall not, Isabel, if you give me love.
ISABELLA	I know your virtue hath a licence in't Which seems a little fouler than it is To pluck on others.
ANGELO	Believe me, on mine honour, My words express my purpose. (2.4.118–49)

CONTINUED

Answers can be found at: www.hoddereducation.co.uk/workbookanswers

(d) Below are two examples of 'Notes to self' from different students who will be responding to AQA-style questions that require comment on a view of the play in relation to an extract and to material elsewhere in the play. Read both notes, highlighting points that you agree with, and then create your own 'Note to self' in relation to such questions on *Measure for Measure*.

Note to self (1)

- Remember that the two parts of the question are separate so keep them separate.

- Keep in mind that most of the marks are for AO1, AO2 and AO3.

- Comment in detail on the extract before going on to write about other parts of the play.

- Pick out particular words and images and explain what they mean.

- Keep in mind what would be happening on stage.

- Try to show that I understand how the characters use language.

- Save comments on contexts and interpretations until the second part of my answer.

- Clarify whether I agree or disagree with the view expressed.

Note to self (2)

- Remember that the two parts of the question are marked as a whole so there is no need to repeat points already made.

- Keep in mind that while most of the marks are for AO1, AO2 and AO3 I do need to gain credit for AO4 and AO5, especially in the second part of my answer.

- When commenting in detail on the extract, look for chances to link with what I plan to say about other parts of the play.

- Pick out particular words and images but, rather than explain what they mean, analyse how they contribute to Shakespeare's dramatic intentions.

- Keep in mind what would be happening on stage so that I can comment on how different audiences might respond.

- Demonstrate my understanding of how and why Shakespeare has given the characters particular uses of language.

- Comment on the context in which 'Measure for Measure' was written and how it might be received by different audiences.

- Always remember that different interpretations are possible.

- Try to engage with a debate on the view expressed by referring to other views, rather than just agreeing or disagreeing.

CONTINUED ➡

....

....

....

....

....

....

....

....

....

....

....

....

....

....

....

....

....

....

KEY SKILLS

Questions requiring a response to a statement have two distinct parts but are marked as a whole, so take the opportunity to demonstrate different skills in different parts of your answer. Focus on specific details of language features and dramatic technique when considering the extract and expect to comment on contexts, comparisons and interpretations when writing about wider aspects of the play. If possible, find ways of linking your specific comments on the extract with your insights into the play as a whole.

Incorporating quotations

12 Which of the tips listed below do you think would **not** be helpful? Put a cross next to any you believe to be bad advice.

A Make sure that quotations are relevant to the point you are making.

B Always quote a full line of verse to show that you understand blank verse.

C Keep them brief – often single words or phrases. It is rarely necessary to quote consecutive lines of dialogue.

D Integrate quotations into your sentences.

E Consider including who says the quotation and, possibly, where broadly it appears in the play.

F Include the line reference for any quotation from the play.

G Try to include quotations you can subsequently analyse and explore.

CONTINUED →

Analysing (AO2)

You need to demonstrate to the examiner that you can analyse the ways in which meanings are created in *Measure for Measure*. This will require you to conduct some close analysis of the effects of language choices, dramatic techniques and structure, as shown in the example below.

13 In the table below, analyse each quotation. You could consider connotations, patterns and links with other parts of the play, and draw on inferences. Where possible, identify any literary techniques Shakespeare is using and comment on their dramatic impact. The first has been done as an example.

QUOTATION
DUKE ... Spirits are not finely touched But to fine issues: nor nature never lends The smallest scruple of her excellence But, like a thrifty goddess, she determines Herself the glory of a creditor, Both thanks and use. (1.1.35–40)
ANALYSIS
At this early stage in the play Shakespeare is conveying subtle messages about future themes and developments. The language of commerce and exchange infuses this sentence and the semantic field of weighing and measuring recurs throughout the play. The Duke, like Nature, is a 'creditor', lending out Angelo and expecting a return. The term 'touch'd' has connotations of gold which is tested by a touchstone, and the alliterative 'smallest scruple' is a unit of measure. When faced with 'fine issues' Angelo's apparently golden character will be found debased by lust and hypocrisy but the Duke, as creditor / god, will call in his loan and gain the glory.
QUOTATION
ISABELLA As much for my poor brother as myself: That is, were I under the terms of death, Th'impression of keen whips I'd wear as rubies, And strip myself to death as to a bed That longing have been sick for, ere I'd yield My body up to shame. (2.4.99–104)
ANALYSIS
....
QUOTATION
ISABELLA O, I do fear thee, Claudio, and I quake Lest thou a feverous life shouldst entertain And six or seven winters more respect Than a perpetual honour. Dar'st thou die? The sense of death is most in apprehension, And the poor beetle that we tread upon In corporal sufferance finds a pang as great As when a giant dies. (3.1.73–9)

CONTINUED ➡

ANALYSIS

....

....

....

....

....

....

....

QUOTATION

CLAUDIO Ay, but to die and go we know not where,
To lie in cold obstruction and to rot,
This sensible warm motion to become
A kneaded clod, and the delighted spirit
To bathe in fiery floods or to reside
In thrilling region of thick-ribbed ice
To be imprisoned in the viewless winds
And blown with restless violence round about
The pendent world, or to be worse than worst
Of those that lawless and incertain thought
Imagine howling; 'tis too horrible.

(3.1.118–28)

ANALYSIS

....

....

....

....

....

....

....

QUOTATION

POMPEY I am as well acquainted here as I was in our house of profession. One would
think it were Mistress Overdone's own house, for here be many of her old
customers. First, here's young Master Rash; he's in for a commodity of brown
paper and old ginger, nine score and seventeen pounds, of which he made five
marks ready money: marry, then ginger was not much in request, for the old
women were all dead.

(4.3.1–7)

CONTINUED ➡

ANALYSIS

....

....

....

....

....

....

....

14 Some exam boards ask questions that require response to a passage and to material elsewhere or to the play as a whole. In responding to passage-based questions you need to focus closely on the language of the passage and on dramatic techniques as well as relating the passage to the play as a whole. Imagine you have been prompted to consider how Isabella is presented in an extract as part of your answer to a question on 'aspects of feminine power'.

(a) Annotate the speech below to show:

- how Shakespeare's language choices show Isabella's character
- how the speech engages the audience in Isabella's plight
- what it shows about Isabella's attitudes
- how she views herself.

ISABELLA   To whom should I complain? Did I tell this
                Who would believe me? Oh, perilous mouths
                That bear in them one and the self-same tongue,
                Either of condemnation or approof,
                Bidding the law make curtsey to their will,
                Hooking both right and wrong to th'appetite
                To follow as it draws. I'll to my brother.
                Though he hath fall'n by prompture of the blood
                Yet hath he in him such a mind of honour
                That had he twenty heads to tender down
                On twenty bloody blocks he'd yield them up
                Before his sister should her body stoop
                To such abhorred pollution.
                Then Isabel live chaste, and brother, die:
                More than our brother is our chastity.
                I'll tell him yet of Angelo's request,
                And fit his mind to death for his soul's rest.
                (2.4.172–88)

(b) Drawing on your annotations, write at least one paragraph analysing how this speech shows 'aspects of feminine power'. Remember to refer closely to the dramatic impact of the language.

....

....

....

CONTINUED

....

....

....

....

....

....

Connotations: the particular associations of a word or phrase.

Historicism: an approach to literature that gives particular weight to specific historical contexts.

Semantic field: a collection of words and phrases relating to a particular aspect of life; for example, Angelo's reference to those who 'coin heaven's image in stamps that are forbid' is from the semantic field of coinage.

Using context (AO3)

You will be expected to show knowledge of relevant historical, social and literary/cultural context. This could relate to Jacobean society or a modern audience's expectations; the important thing is to make sure it is relevant to your line of argument and not just 'bolted on' because you know that you need to mention context.

15 Read this extract from a student essay on the role of Isabella in *Measure for Measure*. What advice would you give the writer about what to keep and what to change? (Bear in mind the exam board expectation that you will be engaging with contexts of gender, power, morality and society as well the contexts of when texts were written and how they have been received.)

There are some strong female characters in Shakespeare, such as Beatrice in 'Much Ado' and Kate in 'The Taming of the Shrew', but Isabella is not quite in their league. She is first presented as the chaste innocent, scheduled for life as a bride of Christ, but we quickly see another side to her character: she catches on straight away that Julietta will be the person pregnant, and her language when describing martyrdom is close to pornographic. Attitudes to men and women and their respective roles, rights and responsibilities have changed over time and are changing now. From a seventeenth-century perspective the expectations of male and female behaviour shown in the play were well established: women were defined by their role, whether as daughters or wives, and were expected to obey their fathers or husbands. The concept of an independent woman, unless she was Queen Elizabeth I, was virtually unknown. Where Isabella is unusual is that we never see her parents and presume they are dead. She can and does decide and speak for herself, except when it comes to marrying the Duke, when her silence speaks volumes.

Possible advice

(a) Keep:

● ....

● ....

● ....

(b) Change:

● ....

● ....

● ....

CONTINUED ➡

Exploring connections across texts (AO4)

16 Depending on your syllabus you may be asked to compare *Measure for Measure* with other texts. Read or watch at least one other Shakespeare play, preferably *Much Ado About Nothing* or *The Tempest*. Make notes on how that play compares with *Measure for Measure* using the table below.

ASPECT	MEASURE FOR MEASURE	OTHER PLAY
What triggers the main action?		
Which themes are explored?		
Where is the play set, and why?		
What are the main patterns of imagery?		
If there are representatives of the law, how are they presented?		
What picture of society is presented?		
What are the comic and tragic elements?		
What image of justice emerges?		
How do the endings compare?		

KEY SKILLS

Comparing *Measure for Measure* with another text (AO4)

If your specification requires you to compare *Measure for Measure* with another text, be sure to adopt a comparative approach throughout your response. Rather than writing about one text and then the other, write about both texts in the same paragraph. Use comparative signposts such as 'similarly' and 'on the other hand'. You should consider comparing:

- form and structure
- different characteristics of language
- dramatic techniques and their impact
- different contexts
- how certain aspects of a critical perspective can be true of one text but less so of the other.

Interpretations (AO5)

Take your critical interpretation further by reading the work of individual critics. If you quote or refer to critics' ideas in the exam, acknowledge them, integrate them into your own argument and use them to develop your own interpretations.

17 Read the four comments below of one critic, Barbara Everett, writing in 2003:

A '*Measure for Measure* is a violent and sophisticated play in which almost nothing happens.'

B '*Measure for Measure* is in its first superlative half made up of debate and dialogue; the play is not merely dark, but abstract, intellectual, argumentative – and the arguments all turn on bodies.'

C 'Authority and goodness are essentially amateur, hypothetical, circumstantial: they are that which does not despise, at need, squalid shifts like bed tricks, or humping about the head of a dead pirate. They are also, since the Duke corrects only that action which he himself initiated, something like an inward process of responsible self-knowledge, self-discovery.'

D 'The Duke's is a fantastically orderly ending for a fantastically disorderly play, one concerned not (as we might expect) with authority but with humility, not (as we might expect) with sex but with sympathy: the imagination that always "leaps over a wall".'

Choose two of the above quotations, (a) one with which you are in broad agreement, and (b) one that you are less sure about. Write a paragraph about each quotation, one paragraph supporting the view expressed, and one challenging the view expressed.

(a) ....

....

....

....

....

(b) ....

....

....

....

....

CONTINUED ➡

18 Identify and highlight the characteristics of more successful answers from the table of features below:

A Made limited reference to Shakespeare's dramatic/poetic methods	B Sustained focus on Shakespeare as a verse dramatist and his dramatic and poetic methods	C Gave due weight to all elements of the question
D Considered and accurate use of context	E Considered 'elsewhere in the play' by selecting relevant detailed references	F Wrote about the characters as though they were real people
G Neglected either the presentation or critical interpretation of the specified issue	H Explored interpretation, i.e. agreed with, disagreed with or debated the given view	I Referred to 'elsewhere in the play' only in generalised or sweeping terms
J Analysed the key words of the given view	K Made inaccurate or sweeping assertions about context	L Looked at the whole extract in detail with relevant reference to the presentation of aspects of the specified theme

Challenge yourself

Put your skills to the test by tackling the question below.

'Typically, texts of the time present women as powerless in the face of male domination.'
In the light of this view, discuss how Shakespeare presents the relationship between Angelo and Isabella in this extract and elsewhere in the play.

ISABELLA	That I do beg his life, if it be sin,
	Heaven let me bear it. You granting of my suit,
	If that be sin, I'll make it my morn-prayer
	To have it added to the faults of mine
	And nothing of your answer.
ANGELO	Nay, but hear me,
	Your sense pursues not mine: either you are ignorant
	Or seem so crafy, and that's not good.
ISABELLA	Let me be ignorant and in nothing good
	But graciously to know I am no better.
ANGELO	Thus wisdom wishes to appear most bright
	When it doth tax itself, as these black masks
	Proclaim an enshield beauty ten times louder
	Than beauty could, displayed. But mark me.
	To be receivéd plain, I'll speak more gross:
	Your brother is to die.
ISABELLA	So.
ANGELO	And his offence is so as it appears
	Accountant to the law upon that pain.

CONTINUED ⏵

ISABELLA	True.
ANGELO	Admit no other way to save his life – As I subscribe not that, nor any other, But in the loss of question – that you, his sister, Finding yourself desired of such a person Whose credit with the judge, or own great place, Could fetch your brother from the manacles Of the all-binding law, and that there were No earthly mean to save him, but that either You must lay down the treasures of your body To this supposed, or else to let him suffer: What would you do?
ISABELLA	As much for my poor brother as myself: That is, were I under the terms of death, Th'impression of keen whips I'd wear as rubies, And strip myself to death as to a bed That longing have been sick for, ere I'd yield My body up to shame.
ANGELO	Then must your brother die.
ISABELLA	And 'twere the cheaper way: Better it were a brother died at once, Than that a sister by redeeming him Should die for ever. (2.4.69–109)

TAKING IT FURTHER

19 Read some (not all!) of the critics listed in the bibliography at the end of this book in a questioning spirit. Ask yourself what their standpoints are, how their approaches influence what they find in the play and how far you agree with them.

Bibliography

Burton, T. I. (2017) 'What a lesser-known Shakespeare play can tell us about Harvey Weinstein', *Vox media*, 15 November.

Chedgzoy, K. (2000) *Measure for Measure,* Northcote House/British Council, Tavistock.

Cook, J. (1983) *Shakespeare's Players*, Harrap, London.

Crowe, A. (2017) *Study & Revise Measure for Measure*, Hodder Education, London.

Dollimore, J. (1985) 'Transgression and surveillance in *Measure for Measure*', *Political Shakespeare: New Essays in Cultural Materialism*, J. Dollimore and A. Sinfield (eds), Cornell University Press, Manchester, pp. 72–87.

Eagleton, T. (1983) *Literary Theory*, Blackwell, Oxford.

Eagleton, T. (1986) *William Shakespeare*, Blackwell, Oxford.

Everett, B. (2003) 'The pirate's head', *Guardian*, 7 January.

Gibbons, B. (ed.) (2006) *Measure for Measure*, Cambridge University Press, Cambridge.

Goldberg, J. A. (2011) 'Power and transgression in *Twelfth Night* and *Measure for Measure*: artifice and ideology as tools of the elite', *Inquiries*, 3(10).

Lanier, G. (1987) 'Physic that's bitter to sweet end: The tragicomic structure of *Measure for Measure*', *Essays in Literature*, 14(1) (Spring), pp. 15–36.

Leavis, F. R. (2008) *The Common Pursuit*, Faber & Faber, London.

Lever, J. W. (ed.) (1965) *Measure for Measure*, Arden edition, Methuen, London.

Rutter, C. (1988) *Clamorous Voices: Shakespeare's Women Today*, The Women's Press, London.

Stead, C. K. (ed.) (1971) *Shakespeare: Measure for Measure*, Casebook series, Palgrave Macmillan, London.

Watts, C. (1986) *William Shakespeare: Measure for Measure*, Penguin, London.

Wilson Knight, G. (1930) *The Wheel of Fire*, Oxford University Press, Oxford.

Wood, N. (ed.) (1996) *Measure for Measure*, Open University Press, Buckingham.

Answers can be found on: www.hoddereducation.co.uk/workbookanswers

The publisher would like to thank the following for permission to reproduce copyright material:

Acknowledgments:

Throughout: William Shakespeare: from 'Measure for Measure' (1623), public domain; **p. 6: G. Lanier**: from 'Physic that's bitter to sweet end: The tragicomic structure of Measure for Measure', *Essays in Literature*, 14(1) (Spring, 1987), pp. 15–36, reprinted with permission of Gregory W. Lanier; **p. 7: C. Watts**: from 'William Shakespeare: Measure for Measure' (Wordsworth Editions, 2005), reproduced under fair usage; **p. 9: B. Everett**: from 'The pirate's head', (*Guardian*, 7 January, 2003), copyright Guardian News & Media Ltd 2018; **p. 43: J. W. Lever**: from 'Measure for Measure (Arden Shakespeare)' (Methuen, 1965), reproduced under fair usage; p. 53: Tara Isabella Burton: from 'What a lesser-known Shakespeare play can tell us about Harvey Weinstein' (Vox Media, 15 November 2017), reprinted with permission of Vox Media, Inc; **p. 54: G. Wilson Knight**: from *The Wheel of Fire* (Oxford University Press, 1930), reproduced under fair usage; **p. 54: J. A. Goldberg**: from 'Power and transgression in Twelfth Night and Measure for Measure: artifice and ideology as tools of the elite', Inquiries, 3(10) (2011), reproduced under fair usage; **p. 58: A. Crowe**: from *Study and Revise for AS/A-level: Measure for Measure* (Hodder Education, 2017), reproduced under fair usage.

Every effort has been made to trace all copyright holders, but if any have been inadvertently overlooked, the Publishers will be pleased to make the necessary arrangements at the first opportunity.

Although every effort has been made to ensure that website addresses are correct at time of going to press, Hodder Education cannot be held responsible for the content of any website mentioned. It is sometimes possible to find a relocated web page by typing in the address of the home page for a website in the URL window of your browser.

Orders: please contact Bookpoint Ltd, 130 Milton Park, Abingdon, Oxon OX14 4SB. Telephone: (44) 01235 827720. Fax: (44) 01235 400401. Lines are open 9.00–17.00, Monday to Saturday, with a 24-hour message answering service. Visit our website at www.hoddereducation.co.uk

ISBN 9781510434998

© Michael Jones 2018

First published in 2018 by
Hodder Education
An Hachette UK Company,
Carmelite House, 50 Victoria Embankment
London EC4Y 0DZ

Impression number   5 4 3 2 1

Year   2022 2021 2020 2019 2018

Cover photo © Cristian Baitg/Vetta/Getty Images

Typeset by Integra Software Services Pvt. Ltd., Pondicherry, India

Printed in Spain

A catalogue record for this title is available from the British Library

HODDER EDUCATION

t: 01235 827827
e: education@bookpoint.co.uk
w: hoddereducation.co.uk

ISBN 978-1-5104-3499-8

MIX
Paper from
responsible sources
FSC™ C104740